"The stories held within this book portray a man I have known for decades—a man who led his church during one of the most difficult times in history to become a true model of caring and compassion. You will be inspired by the ministry of David Crosby and the people of First Baptist New Orleans as they served, like our Lord Jesus, the hurting and displaced in the aftermath of one of the greatest storms of the century. You will be blessed and challenged by the words of Dr. David Crosby."

—DR. FRANK S. PAGE, president and chief executive officer of the Southern Baptist Convention Executive Committee

"I know of no one more qualified to write this manifesto than David Crosby. He loves this vision of holistic ministry, both evangelism and justice, to both souls and bodies. *The Care Effect* gives practical wisdom on how to lead gospel-driven mercy ministry. I pray that thousands will read, and heed, this wise book."

—RUSSELL MOORE, president of the Southern Baptist Ethics & Religious Liberty Commission

"Anyone who accuses the church of being disconnected from its community never met David Crosby and the incredible people of First Baptist New Orleans. With their sleeves rolled up, they demonstrate the gospel weekly as they meet the needs of their neighbors. They show the rest of us what it means to really love other people—in tangible, specific, sacrificial ways. This book is more than their story. It's a call to action for every church to obey Jesus' instructions to love neighbors, enemies, and outsiders. Read it and accept the challenge!"

—DR. JEFF IORG, president, Golden Gate Baptist Theological Seminary

"David Crosby and the congregation of First Baptist New Orleans have focused on the 'heart' of the Gospels . . . loving and caring unconditionally! They have been an inspiration to our city and a beacon of hope and comfort for vulnerable children and families."

—MARY LANDRIEU, former three-term U.S. Senator for Louisiana

"I've been so blessed to be able to work with David Crosby and his congregation on foster care and adoption. They're truly blazing the trail, showing how engaged Christians can make a huge, positive difference in civil society."

—DAVID VITTER, U.S. Senator for Louisiana

"Reverend Crosby is to be commended for his most poignant look at urban problems facing us today and the reality that Jesus is the answer."

—DRAYTON McLANE JR., chairman of McLane Group

"*The Care Effect* reflects David Crosby's ongoing capability of expressing how teachings from Scripture can be applied in meeting the challenges of everyday life in modern society. David recounts poignant experiences in his personal journey from rural West Texas to the culturally diverse community of New Orleans burdened by poverty, despair, crime, and the devastation of Hurricane Katrina. His message of hope and his call to action demonstrate how this good man from Texas has adapted his beliefs and principles to an environment so different from his roots and shown all of us the universal applicability of caring for those in need around us, wherever we are."

—RICHARD C. ADKERSON, president and chief executive officer
of Freeport-McMoRan Inc.

# THE CARE EFFECT

## Unleashing the Power of Compassion

### David Crosby

**NEW HOPE®**
PUBLISHERS
Gospel-Centered. Missions-Driven.

BIRMINGHAM, ALABAMA

New Hope® Publishers
PO Box 12065
Birmingham, AL 35202-2065
NewHopePublishers.com
New Hope Publishers is a division of WMU®.

Library of Congress Cataloging-in-Publication Data

Names: Crosby, David, 1953- author.
Title: The care effect : unleashing the power of compassion / David Crosby.
Description: Birmingham, AL : New Hope Publishers, 2016.
Identifiers: LCCN 2016002597 | ISBN 9781596694712 (sc)
Subjects: LCSH: Church work--Louisiana--New Orleans. | Caring--Religious
 aspects--Christianity. | Compassion--Religious aspects--Christianity. |
 First Baptist New Orleans (Church : New Orleans, La.)
Classification: LCC BV4403 .C76 2016 | DDC 286/.176335--dc23 LC record
available at http://lccn.loc.gov/2016002597

ISBN-10: 1-59669-471-8
ISBN-13: 978-1-59669-471-2

N164111 • 0616 • 3M1

# Contents

# PART THREE: LOVING DEEDS    79

# PART FOUR: DO NOT GIVE UP ON GOOD    135

# SUMMARY: DOING WHAT WE KNOW    171

# Dedication

For the staff and lay members of
First Baptist New Orleans who operate the Care Effect

—ตตต—

# Acknowledgments

Anna Palmer, executive director of Crossroads NOLA, formerly served as missions minister for First Baptist New Orleans (FBNO). She conceived and launched the Care Effect strategy.

Bob Moore, associate pastor of administration at FBNO, helped with the launching of Care Effect and has led our Community Care since its inception.

Christi Gibson, minister of connections at FBNO, helped develop Care Effect and is now leading it for us.

Andrew Crosby, my brother Danny's son, has worked with our mission endeavors for ten years and leads in daily operations for our local missions.

A hundred volunteers deploy from FBNO each week into the neighborhoods and residential institutions of our community. They are the heart, hands, and feet of the ministries of compassion that comprise the Care Effect at FBNO.

# Preface

MY FATHER WAS MY GREATEST TEACHER. BUT HE DID NOT describe to me this relationship between the words and deeds of the gospel.

My pastor brothers have been my closest friends in Christ and treasured companions. But this perspective on the love of neighbor did not emerge in my dialogue with them.

These are not original thoughts, I know. But the rich spiritual journey of my youth did not lead me beside the waters of faith in action. I treasure all that I learned as a child, as a university and seminary student, and as a young pastor. My heritage of faith, however, viewed the written and spoken Word as the primary, if not the exclusive, vehicle of proclamation. Faithful behavior was defined mostly in the negative—what we did not do—rather than in its complementary role in declaring and revealing the good news of Christ.

This understanding of the gospel of Christ formed in me slowly, not all at once. It was drawn for me and from me in the quiet recesses of meditation in God's Word. It was forged and welded in a rich seedbed of pastoral experiences over decades.

And it came to full bloom in the effort to communicate God's love in the perplexing contradiction of my own place, my first missions field, the "city of the saints" and the homicide capital of America.

I kept a pair of blue jeans and a wallet in my office for weeks. If you examine the jeans you can see a perfectly round hole just to the right of the left back pocket. If you pull open the pocket you will see another round hole and on top of that pocket, a rip about two inches long.

The trifold leather wallet has an evident nick on top. If you unfold it you will notice a scar on the inside, a tear on another panel, and a rip about an inch long in the spine of the fold.

The wallet belongs to our friend and First Baptist New Orleans (FBNO) team member, B. J. He was at the Bunny Friend Playground in New Orleans when multiple persons opened fire on the crowd. Seventeen people were wounded, including ten who were under 20 years old. B. J. ran when he heard the burst of gunfire. The person running beside him fell to the ground. B. J. felt the pinch as a bullet struck his wallet, and he thought that he was wounded.

As it turned out, B. J. was unharmed, but his wallet was another story. All its contents were torn up by the bullet that passed through.

Our church staff was stunned when we learned that B. J. had actually been struck by a bullet. We checked with other families we knew when we first heard about the shooting. All of them were safe. Now we learned this.

Bunny Friend Playground is in the Upper Ninth Ward of New Orleans. We helped restore this park after Hurricane Katrina in 2005. We started recreation ministry and tutoring there, and we called it our Bunny Friend ministry. We brought the children to our church. Families who lived nearby became members of our church family.

We are intimately connected to the Bunny Friend Playground. The carnage that occurred there November 22, 2015, is hard for us to process as a congregation. Bunny Friend Playground has been the location of many Backyard Bible Clubs and Vacation Bible Schools.

Living in New Orleans has changed how I think about the world and the gospel. The streets of this city are red with the blood of the slain. The per capita homicide rate is staggering year after year. As I write these words, the murder of a 15-year-old boy, Kevin Thomas, has shaken our ministry team that visits weekly in the juvenile detention center. They knew him and shared the love of Christ with him. And now he is dead. Hundreds of such obituaries were once displayed on the wall in that prison—stories of young men shot in the face or heart or lungs or liver or back or side. Kevin was shot four times fleeing the scene of a drug deal, news reports said. He died on the living room floor in the presence of his mother.

Kevin's story is not an isolated event for those of us who go to work every day in the Big Easy. It is the continuing saga of a city that cannot tamp down its murder rate no matter what it tries to do.

The violence creates grief, fear, and desperation. City leaders welcome the input of anyone with ideas, including pastors. In fact, pastors are repeatedly called to the table by the mayors and police chiefs and sheriffs. "Can houses of worship help us reduce the violence in our city?" they ask. What would you tell them?

Someone commented to me that New Orleans is the most evangelized city in America. Depending on the meaning of "evangelized," they might be right. I suppose at least a million people came to our city in the aftermath of Hurricane Katrina seeking to do good deeds and proclaim the gospel. In fact, New Orleans has been a destination city for missions activities for many years and continues to be so to the present day. The domestic missions board of the Southern Baptist Convention was formed in 1845 in part to evangelize the City of New Orleans.

Simon was an old man when Hurricane Katrina thundered down upon us. He tried to evacuate and sat in his car for hours in gridlocked traffic. He finally called his nephew and said, "I've lived a good, long life, and I am going back home." Simon drowned in his home in Lakeview the next day. I miss him still.

We did not drown. We did not die. We are Katrina survivors. We know what it takes to put a life and community back together. Our memories are not all pleasant, but they are powerful. And they continue to shape the people that we are and will become.

We have not gotten over the great flood. We are still going through it in mind and heart. We live today in light of what we learned about the transitory nature of things and the supreme value of one another.

I take seriously the challenges of poverty and violence in my city. And I struggle to understand what all of this means for me and my church. I ask hard questions and talk to many different individuals about the nature of the proclamation and incarnation of the gospel in my own context.

I am passionate about Jesus as the way, the truth, and the life. Jesus alone is Lord. That is the truth that guides my steps every day. You will see in the pages of this book, though, how my own thinking has changed about the role of loving deeds in the work of the church in this kind of world.

I hope you are asking these tough questions. The cities of the world are growing and will continue to do so. Urban problems are showing up in rural settings as the world gets smaller and technology gives instant access across time zones. How does the good news of the gospel look and sound in "the city that care forgot"?

# PART ONE

# Broken Seams

*You have shaken the land*
*and torn it open; mend*
*its fractures, for*
*it is quaking.*

PSALM 60:2

MY MOTHER ASKED HER GROWN SONS TO FETCH HER NEWLY purchased upright piano. We climbed into Tim's pickup truck and began the search for a farmhouse way off the beaten path.

They were expecting us, that older couple so ready to get rid of the piano. It was old and unbelievably heavy, weathered and faded, but seemed in good condition. The four of us brothers, with slight assistance from the sellers, struggled to load it in the pickup truck. Once it rested in the bed of the truck we all felt there was no way it was going anywhere; it was so heavy, and we did not secure it.

That was our first mistake.

On the way back to the house I realized we were passing right by the business where I needed to deliver my résumé. The chairman of the pastor search committee for Trinity Baptist Church was the managing partner of Medical Plastics Laboratory. I told my brothers we needed to stop for just a second and let me run inside and give him my résumé.

That was our second mistake.

When we turned off the highway into the parking lot, the driveway went sharply down. The pickup rocked and twisted right, and a gust of wind came blowing through. I saw the piano careen, and I gasped.

That was the third mistake.

Tim, who was driving, heard my gasp and guessed that the piano was in jeopardy. I think everything would have been fine if he had not applied the brakes at just the wrong moment.

That was the fatal mistake.

The old piano needed just a little forward momentum to escape the gravity that held it upright. That momentum was delivered when Tim hit the brakes.

I watched in horror through the rear window of the truck cab as the piano fell sideways in slow motion, laid its back on the pickup bed wall, and then turned a perfect flip and tumbled top first to the pavement.

The cast iron soundboard of a standard piano holds 230 strings under a combined 18 tons of tension. The crash of the piano was stunning. Each one of the 88 hammers must have struck simultaneously when the top lid hit the asphalt. The boom startled people in the buildings nearby. They ran to the windows and flung open the doors to see what had happened.

We jumped out of the pickup and surveyed the damage. The piano had simply come undone. Every seam had popped, and every bond had broken. What remained was a pile of wood on the pavement that did not resemble a piano in any way.

We picked up the pieces—maybe a hundred of them—and put them back in the pickup bed. We couldn't leave the debris of an old piano in the middle of the parking lot. When we were done, not a single piece rose above the level of the pickup walls. Mother's piano was a pile of rubble.

I glanced over my shoulder at the office door as we picked up those broken pieces. This was not the way I had intended to introduce myself to the chairman of the pastor search committee. I delivered my résumé to him before we left, and he had missed the whole disaster and asked no questions of me. The church decided to call me as their pastor, but I did not mention the piano incident for many years. I felt like a numskull.

We drove the ruined piano to our parents' house in silence. The remains of our mother's purchase shivered against the metal bed of the pickup like a load of firewood.

Tim backed up the pickup to the back porch. What else could we do? We propped open the screen door. Mother stood grimly, not speaking, as the four of us made several trips each, carrying the pieces of her piano into the porch and depositing them carefully on the floor.

The shadows were taking over in the porch when we finished our task and got ready to leave. The piano was a pile of wood in the middle of the porch.

"That's $200 down the drain," I thought but did not say as I apologized again to Mom. I gave her a hug and left her still standing in the porch with her hands on her hips and her lips tight.

Weeks later I made another visit to my parents' home. "What did you do with that broken piano?" I asked my mother, and she took me to the porch.

15

There it stood, upright as ever, fully collected and reassembled. I was stunned. I touched the keys and heard the strings sound in tune.

"How can this be?" I asked, amazed.

"Dad and I glued it back together," she said proudly. "We've been playing it."

The old piano was heavy because it was made of the finest oak wood, mother said. They restored the finish, sanding each piece and coating it with polyurethane. "It was actually easier to do with the piano in pieces," she said with a smile.

## LEARNING THE DEPTH OF CARE

John Burris was funny and likable though no one ever suggested he was perfect. He was rough and tough and built like a bulldozer. He would run over you on the basketball court and laugh when you objected.

John's fingers were so thick I marveled that he could actually play any stringed instrument. He couldn't slip my wedding band on his little finger. When you first gripped his hand you would swear that it was swollen from some injury or bee sting. His whole body was that way—thick and hard and strong. He dribbled that basketball on one side of his body and plowed through to the goal with the other, bouncing all of us out of the way.

He was born that way, I am sure. His three sons have the same square build. But he was also honed that way by the hemp lassoes that were always in his hands and the wild horses on the other end. He trained horses for a living, and he followed the rodeo circuit when he had enough cash in his pocket to hit the road.

Willie, John's youngest son and my contemporary, won a calf-roping contest while we were still in high school. He couldn't keep the money because doing so would make him a professional athlete and ineligible for high school play. He wanted to play football for Pottsville High his senior year, so he donated the money to build the basketball court that became the hub of youth activities in our part of Mills County.

We moved the metal folding chairs from our youth Sunday School class most Sunday and Wednesday evenings and set them up along the concrete slab in the back yard of Center City Baptist Church. If it was mid-summer and the sun was still hot, we might set them in the shade of a grove of trees between the red brick Baptist church and the yellow brick Methodist church. Janet and I said our vows in the Baptist church, then walked across a dusty lane and had our reception at the Methodist church.

People used to think Center City was the geographical center of Texas. They actually built a rock wall around a twisted old live oak tree just south of State Highway 84 at the solitary crossroad that comprises all of Center City. While I was a high school senior and college freshman, our family lived just 100 yards or so from that live oak tree. I had nine siblings at the time, and the two-bedroom frame house was too small for all of us. My three oldest brothers and I cleaned up an abandoned building once used by the telephone company and turned it into a bedroom with four Army cots, one on each wall, and a dirt path through the trees to the house. I slept every night at the center of Texas.

Or so I thought until I learned that the geographical center of Texas had been recalculated and lay 20 miles to the west.

When I think of Center City now, I do not think of the center of Texas but of the center of faith and church and God's will for my life. John Burris was the center of Center City for me as a boy. The church that let us tear up the backyard, pour concrete, knock out walls, and wreak general havoc on their facility—that was the center.

The center is the place where people love you, where they teach you how to play the guitar and dribble a basketball. The center is that moment in your life when someone who follows Jesus drops to their knees, washes your feet, and you begin to understand that the basin and the towel are the tools of the gospel.

Leon Wilson scared me from the moment I met him. Maybe it was that obvious injury, a scar where his left eye should have been.

"I lost it in a barroom," he told me with gravel and pride in his voice. The wounded eye socket was part of his mystique. He had compensated for the loss of sight on that side by tilting his head slightly to the left and lifting up the good eye, centering it over his body.

Leon killed people. He told me so. I don't know how many. I thought about that when I saw him walking toward my office, swaying in the rhythm of a stiff gait, square build and hard as a brick wall.

His steps were heavy on the tile floor. He rapped a knuckle on my door and pushed in when I responded. He wore an overcoat when the weather turned lousy and the mist rolled into the pine forests of East Texas. He seemed in a hurry, like someone was pursuing him, and he was nervous as he talked.

"I've done some terrible things, Preacher," he said, standing in front of my desk, ignoring my motion to a chair, dispensing with any niceties. "People would kill me if they could."

He pushed back the right side of his overcoat, exposing a battered leather holster with the ivory handle of a Colt .45 protruding.

"I carry it everywhere I go." He stood for a moment, silent, then turned quickly and disappeared through the door and into the hall. I swiveled in my chair and watched through the window as his hunched form, gray in the half-light of dusk, rocked down the sidewalk toward his old pickup truck. He roared out of the church parking lot in a minute, and I was alone again in the stillness of that little office.

My Bible was open in front of me, but my mind was searching the darkening sky outside, looking for answers to the puzzle of this man.

"Leon, what's up with you?" I thought.

I recognized the gun he wore on his hip. I saw it disassembled on the coffee table the first time I ever saw Leon. I shuddered in my chair as I remembered Leon's dog. I thought it was going to kill me. It charged as I approached the screen door, launched into the air toward my throat, and closed its mouth with a snap and turned when a single order issued through the door.

I wasn't even sure it was the right house. Directions were not easy to follow in the maze of unmarked dirt roads that penetrated the pine forests. I was about to give up and turn around when I caught a glimpse of the old two-story house, paint peeling, weathered boards, sitting like a big wooden box in a small clearing, looking like part of the forest.

Someone in the church had given me his name and said he needed help. That's really all I knew.

I knocked on the screen door. It rattled loosely. The mesh was rusted and torn. I heard a sound from the inside of the house, something like "come in" or "it's open," and I pulled on the handle.

Down a long, unlit hallway, I saw a man working on something with both hands in the dim light of a lamp. He was sitting alone in the middle of a sunken couch, his head and shoulders bent over a coffee table. His booted feet were planted wide, his elbows resting on his knees. He was scrutinizing something.

He did not rise to greet me, but he did look up when I stepped into the living room. He held in two rough hands the barrel and action of a handgun. Its other parts were scattered on the coffee table. I guessed that he was cleaning it.

He lifted his hand, and I caught the scent of gun oil. I shook his hand, and he motioned to a chair. We talked as it grew dark outside. He reassembled the pistol. He wanted to know about my faith, what it meant to trust in Christ for salvation. He got right to the point.

And he told me his story, the part he chose to tell, the part that helped me know who he really was—working security for dangerous people running contraband and whorehouses. He had lived all of his 60 years in that world of shadows, brawls, and broken bottles. He lost his eye there, and his innocence, but he did not want to lose his soul, if he could help it.

He had married late in life. His wife believed in Christ as Lord. He wanted what she had—inner peace and confidence about the future. He bowed his head and talked to God, asking for forgiveness and opening his life to Christ.

We baptized him in front of the congregation, and he attended worship with regularity.

Leon became my friend.

And then he became a cancer patient. The cancer moved fast. It took him down, pinned him to the hospital bed. The doctors said he had days to live.

I went by the hospital one morning to see Leon just hours before he died. He was lucid and eager to tell me what he had experienced the night before.

"Jesus came to see me," he said excitedly. "He stood at the foot of my bed all night. Any time I woke up and looked, He was there."

I don't have to explain who or what Leon saw at the foot of his bed in the hospital that night. A vision of His presence sounds to me like a gift Jesus might give to one He loved. I know that Leon had placed his life in the hands of Jesus Christ as Lord, and he died with a peace that things were right between him and God.

Does our God care for people who work security in dangerous places, even murderers? Yes, He does. Does Jesus watch over thugs-turned-disciples? Yes, indeed. We often come to Him bent down with the weight of guilt and shame and fear on our souls. We come because we are instructed: "Cast all your anxiety on him because he cares for you" (1 Peter 5:7).

Leon discovered that God cared for him despite his ugly past. He cast himself upon the mercy of God at God's own invitation. And he experienced the life-giving relationship with Christ as Savior that is the only path to real peace.

I was 22 years old when I was Leon's pastor. I was just learning about the power of God's love in us. And I was experiencing the power of our love unleashed toward those around us. This is *The Care Effect*.

## SHINE LIKE STARS

Providentially, I attended seminary in New Orleans. Southwestern Baptist Theological Seminary in Fort Worth was a far more natural choice geographically and the choice of my family and friends. But I ended up in New Orleans thanks to a fellow pastor and the kindness of the president of the seminary. Once in New Orleans, I made a living by working as a reporter for the city desk of *The Times-Picayune* and serving a church in Mississippi on the weekends.

As soon as I finished seminary, I moved my family back to Texas and began to work on a doctorate in the School of Religion at Baylor University. For 16 years, I was pastor to three Texas congregations, including First Baptist Church of Temple, Texas.

We designed and built a house on 41 acres of black land east of Temple. I could see the stock tank from the back porch and the line of trees along a creek that ran across the north and eastern perimeters of our land. Coyotes howled at night, and raccoons scoured the yard and porches for anything edible.

I studied the night skies above El Paso as a boy. I saw the handiwork of God in the world outside my bedroom window—in the quiet beauty of Orion's Belt suspended above the Franklin Mountains. Even now that particular constellation gives me a sense of place and peace.

Encountering God in the natural world, the coyote's wail, and the orange glow at dawn, became a way of life for me. Maybe I have a low amazement threshold, but everywhere I turn I am startled by the beauty and majesty of God written into His world. My spiritual life was shaped by biblical and natural theology before I knew the terms.

Our home outside of Temple was a perfect place to see the stars. I often walked the long driveway at night craning my neck toward the marvelous tapestry space.

When the pastor search committee from First Baptist New Orleans inquired, we told them we were not interested. I had to hear from God about going back to New Orleans. I was just not disposed to do it.

We finally made a visit to New Orleans at the invitation of the committee. I could not sleep. At four o'clock in the morning I stepped out on the balcony of our hotel room on the 11th floor and looked for the stars. I could not see even one.

Then I looked down, and twinkling lights from the city stretched from the foot of our hotel out before me as far as I could see. And God said, "These are your stars now." The words of Philippians 2:14–16 came to mind: "Do everything without grumbling or arguing, so that you may become blameless and pure, 'children of God without fault in a warped and crooked generation.' Then you will shine among them like stars in the sky as you hold firmly to the word of life." I felt God saying to me, "I want you to come to New Orleans and help My people shine like stars as they hold forth the Word of life."

This assignment came from God, helping His people in the city shine like stars. It was a specific word from God to me. The certainty of my calling keeps me going and calms my heart when things get tough.

Some assignments in life require the certainty of God's call, the specific word from Him. My call to be pastor of First Baptist New Orleans was one of those assignments.

Helping hardworking families achieve home ownership was another one.

Think about this with me: God prepared His church to build houses for those in need right *before* Hurricane Katrina flooded what The Data Center has calculated as 134,000 houses in New Orleans. Would you say that was coincidence or providence?

If it was providential and God was preparing us for the storm, then God really does care very much about neighbors and their houses.

## GOD TOLD US TO BUILD HOUSES

Something was happening in New Orleans prior to the great storm that was truly a word from God. It came months beforehand in the fall of 2004. It had nothing to do with meteorology or astrology and everything to do with compassion and conviction.

Because God spoke His Word to us, the most hopeful place in New Orleans after the storm was a place that came to be known as Musicians' Village. That project by Habitat for Humanity International and New Orleans Area Habitat for Humanity was destination #1 for every dignitary who came to visit our city, including President George W. Bush.

Musicians' Village really began in the fall of 2004 as the Baptist Crossroads Project. People of faith had mobilized to launch a great home-building effort in our city. And for that reason—and that reason alone—the corner of Alvar and Roman streets became a beacon of hope. Thousands of visitors to the devastated city came to see a beautiful community of multi-colored homes in a debris-strewn wasteland.

The existence of this community was the direct result of a word from God.

My wife, Janet, and I went to California mostly to see the giant redwood forests—and because I needed to stick at least my toe in Nevada so that I could say I had been in all 50 of the United States. Our trip included five days at a Christian camp, a visit to San Francisco and Golden Gate Baptist Theological Seminary, and two days on the Nevada side of Lake Tahoe.

"I'm going to see the largest and one of the oldest living things on Planet Earth," I announced to Michelle in the church foyer, her four children gathered around her. I knew she had just turned 40 years old.

"I saw that tree when I was a little girl," she said hesitantly, smiling.

"It was a lot smaller then," I quipped—and ran, chuckling.

A couple weeks later, we wound through the mountains near the coast of northern California. I had already stood in a grove of redwoods and stared upward in wonder, tracing their ascent toward the heavens. I bowed my head in the midst of those mighty trunks and acknowledged again the glory and greatness our Creator God.

As we cruised through the mountains, I listened to a radio Bible teacher commenting on the difference between the Greek words *logos* and *rhema*, both translated "word" in English Bibles. I had taught that lesson before.

*Logos* is the eternal Word of God, true at all times and places. "God is love" would be such an eternal word (see 1 John 4:8). *Rhema* is God's word for a specific situation and applicable to that time and place alone. The Apostle Paul received such a specific word when God delivered to him what we know as the "Macedonian call." In a vision, Paul heard someone from Macedonia who said, "Come over to Macedonia and help us" (Acts 16:9). This word from the Holy Spirit was intended for a certain time and place. Paul immediately obeyed the heavenly vision, and the gospel of Christ was carried westward in dramatic fashion. Much of the history of the expansion of Christianity in the first century may be traced to this specific word from God to go to Macedonia.

I was driving that California highway and reflecting on this distinction between *logos* and *rhema* when the truth struck me like a lightning bolt from heaven. We had received a *rhema*—a specific word from God—during the months before Hurricane Katrina. Even though it had been a year, and 31 houses had already been built, the full significance of that truth had never dawned on me.

"God spoke to me," I said to myself over and over again as I negotiated the curves in the road. "God told me to build houses," I said out loud. Janet looked up from her book and nodded her head.

This truth of God's certain word to me was full of meaning and dramatic implications for my personal walk with God and the rest of my pastoral ministry.

I knew that God had called us to love our neighbors. I knew that deeds of kindness and concern were part of following Jesus. Therefore, I knew that helping families achieve homeownership was a good and loving work consistent with the character and calling of God.

But I wasn't absolutely certain that "build houses" was a specific word from God just for me. I am not accustomed to having God tell me things like this—a specific instruction to accomplish some concrete task. I always couched my spiritual inclinations with the proviso, "I feel led to . . ." It seemed too arrogant and arbitrary for a pastor to announce that he had heard a specific word from God to go do a certain thing—unless that certain thing was clearly spelled out in Scripture. It seemed to me to be wide open to abuse—and used as a tool for manipulating others.

A good friend and deacon spoke to me. "Pastor, do you really think that our church should be building houses?" It seemed to him to be outside the mission and ministry of our church. I went to God again in prayer. I sensed in my soul that we should do this good work. I spoke to the congregation and told them of my earnest prayer for God's direction and my great sense of peace in proceeding with the plan.

I shared the idea of building 40 new homes with pastors who have been my friends for many years. Some of them expressed honest concerns.

"Building houses is not really the work of the church," some said. "Where does it say that we should do that in the Bible?"

"What about 'I was a stranger, and you took me in,'" I mused out loud (Matthew 25:35). But I knew that what I felt called to do was too specific to claim a direct biblical mandate.

Some pastors were concerned that the project did not seem to directly benefit the church.

"Will these new homeowners be Christians?" they asked. "It makes more sense to provide homes for God's people so they can be witnesses in that neighborhood."

"No," I replied. "Our partnership with Habitat will not allow that kind of discrimination. Besides, this project is about following Jesus' parable of the Good Samaritan. The Good Samaritan loved his neighbor without regard to his religious affiliation or future religious prospects" (see Luke 10:25–37).

Their feedback sent me back to God in prayer, pleading for Him to show me if this was not the right way. But I felt a strong sense in my soul that this is what God wanted us to do. I stood before the church in May of 2005. I opened my Bible and preached from the parable of the Good Samaritan. I told the congregation that I felt led to engage in this unusual work, and I believed that God would use it for His glory and to exalt the Savior in our city.

We had a kickoff Sunday in our church for the home-building project on June 5, 2005. Everyone seemed inspired and challenged. We had broad support within the leadership of the congregation, and many churches were already interested in helping. We launched the website for Baptist Crossroads.

The church and our partners were enthusiastic in their support, but I continually checked with God about our direction. Truthfully, I believed it was a good idea—even an inspired idea. But I could not begin to understand how truly God had spoken this word until after the great flood of New Orleans on August 29, 2005.

God did not tell us about the flood. Only God knew that the flood was coming. But God did tell us to build houses. God told us to do something we as a church had never done before in order to prepare for something we had never experienced.

Five vacant city blocks were discovered and secured in the Upper Ninth Ward before the storm in anticipation of the Baptist Crossroads Project. It was "one of the largest building blitzes by a single denomination in the history of Habitat for Humanity anywhere in the world," according to the director of the local chapter, who told me this as we stood together, looking over those vacant lots owned by the public school system. All buildings had been razed years earlier.

We determined that we would build 40 homes in ten weeks in the summer of 2006 with 3,000 volunteers from churches all over the country. Most of the funding was in place before Hurricane Katrina, and thousands of volunteers were already committed to come.

Then came the terrible storm and the failure of the levees on the interior canals in New Orleans. Some people call it the greatest natural disaster in the history of the United States. Others call it the greatest engineering failure in the history of the U.S. Corps of Engineers. Some call it a judgment from God.

Overnight, the city with the worst housing stock in America became the city with the least housing stock. I watched by television from our evacuation perch in a hotel in Hot Springs, Arkansas, as the saltwater rushed through the levee breaches and the City of New Orleans became part of the sea. And I began to realize that the home-building venture we had planned was something in a different category, a word of great weight and promise. I began to believe that God spoke this word to me, though I did not yet understand it to be His *rhema* for our time of need.

And I knew that 40 homes would not be near enough.

## REFLECTIONS

1. What is the distinction between the Greek words *logos* and *rhema*? How is each translated into English?
2. Is the Apostle Paul unique in receiving the Macedonian call? Who else received specific instructions from God?
3. Can you think of a time in your own church experience when your congregation felt they had received a specific word from God? What was it?
4. Have you ever experienced a specific word from God? If so, what was it?

## CHURCH SHOULD BE MORE THAN A DESTINATION

The physician was busy studying a computer screen, reading reports and looking at graphs. We had met him once before. Janet and I both liked him. He was kind, communicative, humble, and wise.

The thyroid looked about like it did last year, he said, and he was not concerned about any malignancy. But he would order a biopsy just to be sure.

We were pleased, of course. Janet's bout with cancer several years earlier frightened us both and made us more cautious. This was a good report.

"So, do people still go to church?" the doctor asked, scrolling through reports and making notes. He did not look up.

"Oh, yes," I replied. "Many people are active in our churches." In fact, I had just read the results of a survey from the *Journal for the Scientific Study of Religion* that estimated 60 million Americans attended church on any given Sunday. The doctor was a little surprised, I think.

"That's interesting," he said, and scribbled another note on his pad.

The physician's question was a little curious to me. He did not expand on it or explain—just left it out there for consideration: "Do people still go to church?"

Maybe he had a genuine interest in my answer, or maybe he was making a comment with a question. Maybe he thought people were outgrowing the church, that declining attendance indicated failing faith.

"I mean, the churches are dealing with changing circumstances," I continued, hoping to engage him further in this conversation. "Most of us used to live in rural communities where everyone knew everyone. Churches thrived there. Now most of us live in cities where we are often anonymous. Churches are not usually as central to social life in the city as they were in the country."

He responded with a muffled acknowledgment.

"But people are grateful for the gift of life, and want to give God praise," I said. "Many churches are strong and growing."

He swiveled his chair toward us and said his assistant would be in shortly to schedule the biopsy. And he was gone.

"Going to church" is not what it used to be. In fact, the church may not be the destination it once was in these United States. Church attendance remains remarkably strong, but many of us remember a time and place when our churches dominated the social landscape. Such is not the case today.

Maybe the doctor's question, "Do people still go to church," indicates a fundamental problem—church perceived as a destination.

The physician's question was not, "Do churches still go to the needy?" People in general do not perceive the church to be going anywhere.

People go to church. Churches don't go to people. We would never really think to reverse the question. The church in rural America sits at the crossroads with easy access from all directions just like a major retail outlet. The rule is "location, location, location."

That's not wrong. It's right. Church buildings need to be visible and accessible. That's certainly better for the churches than being invisible and inaccessible.

What if the church's visibility was about its work in the community? What if its accessibility was about its presence among neighbors in need? What if we reversed the mindset that church is a destination and instead conceived of the church as an air compressor that gathers and compresses for the purpose of strategic release aimed to make a big difference?

What if actively loving our neighbors became the reputation and perception of the churches in our communities?

People want to do something. The expert in the law asked Jesus, "What must I do to inherit eternal life?" (Luke 10:25). Then Jesus told him the story of the Good Samaritan. The story is certainly about doing something.

Jesus taught us about faith in God. "The work of God is this: to believe in the one he has sent" (John 6:29). Jesus is not departing from faith in the parable of the Good Samaritan. He is illustrating the nature of true faith.

Faith is more verb than noun, more motion than emotion, more doing than thinking. Faith is not a destination so much as a way to journey.

The Apostle Paul declared, "The only thing that counts is faith expressing itself through love" (Galatians 5:6). That is exactly what was going on with the Good Samaritan. Faith was expressed through love of neighbor.

## ONE TERRIFIC BLOW

One terrific blow, upside down, and the old glue gave way at virtually every seam, reducing the oak piano to its component parts. Very few nails or screws were used in its construction. The instrument was crafted for assembly with wooden pins and glue. I still consider the piano's destruction a tragedy perpetrated by a truckload of bonehead brothers. But in the end, it was a miracle!

We are solitary individuals endowed with the capacity for abstract thought. We have an interior life of mind and heart that is infinitely complex and both intellectual and intuitive. We desire to know and be known, but we cannot fully share with anyone who we truly are. We are beings in process, developing morally and mentally, self-aware, but not fully aware even of ourselves. As the subject of experiences, we know life uniquely. We initiate activities. We feel things deeply. We sense distance and separation.

We overcome this solitude by establishing connections with other people. Although we cannot tell anyone everything that goes on inside of us, we can share with others the stories of our lives, hear their stories, and learn to care for one another. If we do not do this, we live in a monotone world. If we reach out to others, we begin to experience the rich diversity, hear the amazing harmony, and see the spectacular kaleidoscope of life in community with significant others.

Life at the highest level happens at these seams. A vital part of recovery from disaster and loss is working on the seams—restoring the connections with others.

Every life has a routine. You shop at the local grocery store. You fill up with gas at the Shell station near the off-ramp. You work out at a gym not far from your house. You get your hair cut, your nails done, and your pets groomed at local establishments. Your pediatrician, gynecologist, dentist, dermatologist, and chiropractor have their offices nearby. The drugstore and dry cleaners you frequent are on your route to work. You develop connections with people. Life happens in the dynamic of these relationships.

Hurricane Katrina took the City of New Orleans, dumped it on its head, and busted every seam. It reduced our city to a pile of rubble and broke virtually every bond that held us together. In the vast footprint of the flood zone, 100 square miles of the city itself, every house and car was flooded and every business drowned—150,000 houses and 18,000 businesses.

The neighbors were not returning, they said. The medical specialists were relocating permanently. The old barber did not evacuate and drowned in his house. The gym would lie in shambles for years.

We assemble our lives by establishing connections with people around us. Soon we know the name of the young woman across the counter who dry cleans our clothes or rings us up at the store. We hear the stories of our neighbors and get to know them. We care for their pets while they are out of town.

Now the people, the pets, and the businesses were gone. Many would never return. Others would take years to come back.

The greatest grief we suffered as a result of Hurricane Katrina was not the loss of property but the loss of relationships and the destruction of a way of life.

A distraught mother told me that she got lost looking for the home she lived in for 12 years. The street signs were all gone. Other than large trees, all the vegetation in the flood zone was dead. Vehicles had floated from their parking places. Sheds collapsed. Shifting currents of flood waters carried familiar landmarks out of view.

All the green yards and shrubs were now brown and dead. All the parks were silent. All the schools were gone along with the children. It was months after Hurricane Katrina before we had a baby in our church nursery.

Life came apart at the seams, reduced by the flood to a pile of rubble. We all got lost trying to find home.

Franklin Avenue Baptist Church is a predominantly black congregation, the largest Southern Baptist congregation in Louisiana. They worshiped and worked with us in the facilities of First Baptist New Orleans for two and a half years after the great flood while they restored their church buildings. When they departed, they gave us a spectacular gift—a new Steinway grand piano. We were playing the old pianos that were damaged by months of uncontrolled heat and humidity.

Our worship leader, Robert Comeaux, and our keyboardist, Kirk Branch, traveled to New York to visit the Steinway factory. Robert told me it was a great experience to see how the various parts of the piano were fashioned and how it was all assembled.

I see that Steinway on our platform, and I think about Pastor Fred Luter and the "Franklinites" who continue to be our friends and partners in ministry. The currents of the great flood washed us into one another, and we were all the richer for it.

The piano is a work of art, a great reminder that life is more than the sum of its parts.

Life takes many unexpected turns. Sometimes it feels like things are "coming apart at the seams," and sometimes they do, as a matter of fact. The connections are lost.

The command to love our neighbor often catches us in awkward moments and uncomfortable places. We find ourselves in great need of healing and restoration. We feel that we are at a low point in our own journey. Helping someone else seems to be a stretch when we are in so much need ourselves.

But we serve a great God who is able to restore what has been broken, to replace what has been lost, and to reconfigure the pieces of our lives to achieve His majestic purpose in us. We lay before Him the pieces of our broken piano, and He is able to accomplish the miracle of restoration. We cooperate with God in this restorative process by keeping the Great Commandment in the forefront of our lives: love God, love neighbor. God fully restores us by removing impurities that weaken the bonds of love. He helps us reconnect in love to those around us, restoring broken relationships and developing new ones.

Keeping the Great Commandment means that your life keeps going forward, getting richer. Don't ever give up on love no matter what you have lost. Love is the tie that binds. Life happens at the seams.

## WE HOVER ABOVE THE RUBBLE

Shapes were buried in the water below us. Large, colorful forms distorted by shimmering waves lined the neutral ground of West End Boulevard for miles. Our medians are "neutral ground" because the fierce loyalty to your neighborhood is suspended at these seams. Looking down I knew only West End had a neutral ground that wide.

Ahead of us was the ribbon of Interstate 610 with the facilities of First Baptist New Orleans just beyond it, completely surrounded by gentle waves. We would soon set down the helicopter on a section of the parking lot that had emerged from the flood. Eleven days after the storm, the church facility was an island in the sea. All residences and businesses for miles around the church were flooded. Every street was a bayou, including Interstate 10 that dove under the Mounds Street railroad trestle just west of the church and was now a lake 15 feet deep.

*My view from the helicopter.*

Thousands of above-ground tombs were underwater in Greenwood Cemetery next to the church. A forest of stone crosses stood above the flood, their reflections moving in the water.

To the right of our flight was the 17th Street Canal that failed in the storm. Lake Pontchartrain lay behind us to the north. To the left, looking east, the housetops were captured in glistening floodwaters as far as the eye could see.

A parade of military helicopters thumped the air along the perimeter of the south shore of the lake. Enormous bags of sand swung beneath them, part of a futile effort to plug the hole in the levee and stop the sea's invasion of the city.

"Cars," I said to myself and then to the pilot over the headphones. "Those are cars beneath the surface." Part of the normal evacuation process was parking vehicles on high ground. Residents along West End Boulevard parked hundreds of vehicles on the neutral ground. They were among the hundreds of thousands of vehicles ruined by Hurricane Katrina.

In ten days, West End Boulevard would finally be dry. In six months, its entire three-mile median, almost a thousand feet wide, would become a dump site. The storm debris would be segregated into sections of ruined appliances, trees and vegetation, furniture and household goods, and the soggy trash of gutted houses—insulation, Sheetrock, and lumber. The piles would be 30 feet high stretching from side to side and running the entire length of the median.

Even at high tide the water did not cover the church parking lot. The National Guard had set up camp there, I noticed from the air. The pilot set the helicopter down on the parking lot of the church, and we were immediately approached by armed military personnel. We explained who we were and why we were there.

The church facility had not taken on rising water. Our construction team had covered the building site with two feet of fill dirt before starting construction. That fill had lifted the new facility out of the flood. We had occupied it only 15 months earlier.

I followed two soldiers with lights on their M-16 rifles. Electricity would not be restored for months. They entered every room in the church facility before they gave me permission to retrieve the things I needed. We found two dogs in the preschool area with their food scattered in the lobby. Someone who slept on my office couch had scrawled a thank you note and left a telephone number on a chalkboard.

Half of my staff did not return. I know they did the right thing. Half of the congregation relocated permanently. I could have bailed. But I strapped myself in literally and figuratively when we lifted off the parking lot for the return flight back to Texas.

The Spirit of God hovered over the floodwaters on that day so filled with shock and awe. Anticipation rattled around in my soul, though I could not identify it on the flight. I was overwhelmed, but God was up to something. I was tumbling in the hurricane, but God, who rides upon the storm, was about to create something out of the chaos.

A million volunteers flooded into the Gulf Coast in those first 30 months after Hurricane Katrina's landfall. The Red Cross mounted the largest relief effort in its 124-year history, receiving and spending nearly $2.2 billion total during the aftermath of the 2005 Atlantic hurricane season, which included hurricanes Katrina, Rita, and Wilma.

Hundreds of thousands of church members from thousands of churches came to help the people of New Orleans in the wake of the storm. I suspect it was the greatest effort of voluntary assistance in the history of the American church and surely the greatest in the history of my own denomination, the Southern Baptist Convention.

Our church facility, like many others, became a disaster relief center with the Red Cross, the Salvation Army, and Southern Baptist Disaster Relief, the "yellow caps," working together to serve thousands of meals and distribute tons of water, food, and cleaning supplies.

More than 200 church members of First Baptist New Orleans gave significant time and effort to the building of new homes in cooperation with Habitat for Humanity. Eventually the partnership between our congregation and Habitat produced 91 new homes. More than 100 members joined in the Home Recovery Ministry that helped 1,100 homeowners, mostly by gutting flooded homes. We deployed 21,000 volunteers to projects initiated by our own congregation.

I continue my own efforts to integrate all the experiences of Katrina and her aftermath into my life of faith in Christ and my work as a gospel minister. I was predisposed, I think, toward a certain direction, but I rode the wave of Katrina into a new perspective on the work of Christ's church.

The post-Katrina world of tumbled and jumbled possessions and connections continues to be a fertile field for the germination of new ideas in all disciplines—including theology. God's purpose in our pain is always redemptive, regardless of the cause. Therefore this chastening of the Lord distinguishes our city's believing population as worthy of God's special attention for His own eternal purpose. He only chastens those He loves.

This amounts to a confession that the rod of God has fallen upon us. But it goes beyond the reality of judgment to the purposes of God. "Katrina" means purification. I believe that God was purifying His church in the midst of this storm.

People of faith have been hoping for and praying for a great turning to God as a result of the storm. I think that has happened, but not in the way we would have predicted or maybe preferred. God's purpose in this storm had much more to do with His church than with the lost world. The flood did not touch Bourbon Street and the famous flesh markets of our city. Rather, the flood destroyed hundreds of churches and the homes of thousands of followers of Jesus Christ. The storm reduced our already struggling congregations to tiny remnants of our pre-Katrina selves.

And the storm washed us out of our pews and into the streets and lanes of our city. This is the revival of the church that has already happened and continues to this day in the City of New Orleans and across the nation. Thousands of churches are rediscovering the central role of deeds of compassion and love in the proclamation of the gospel. Young believers in our churches are drawn to this "hands-on" ministry that incarnates the good news in the places where they live and work.

I believe this was the purpose of God for many reasons. God rides upon the storm. God spoke to Job out of the storm.

And God has spoken to us.

God is speaking even now through the great devastation of Hurricane Katrina. His message is for all people, especially those who claim to follow Christ as Lord. We who have been the beneficiaries of this great outpouring of love and volunteer support—we have a word to share.

The certainty of this word from God transcends the present crisis. God was preparing many of us for the flood that only He knew would come. The preparation was evident only in hindsight.

Many self-proclaimed prophets have predicted the devastation of New Orleans. A friend called me in 2011 to warn me that New Orleans would be destroyed in 2012. According to teachers he was listening to, the planets were aligning and the sea would rise until New Orleans was 600 feet under water. He plead with me to leave the city. I declined. I do not make decisions based on religious interpretations of the movements of heavenly bodies. That would be astrology. If an astronomer—a scientist—tells me we are about to be struck by a meteor, that's a different story.

The predicted disaster—like many others before it—did not occur. We should note this truth and take future religious predictions of a similar nature with two or three grains—or boxes—of salt.

No modern-day prophet prepared us for the devastation of Hurricane Katrina. The Prophet Isaiah helped, though, when he said, "By his wounds we are healed" (Isaiah 53:5). The Apostle Paul also helped when he wrote, "In all things God works for the good of those who love him" (Romans 8:28).

What was God's word to His church caught in the great devastation of Hurricane Katrina? What is God's word to those who came to help? Does God have a word for His people in general?

I will try to answer those questions and clearly establish how God's people can and must respond to the Father's heart as He goes about chastening and pruning His church.

## GOD SPEAKS IN THE STORM

A middle-aged woman attended worship at our church in the summer of 2015. She sat up front on the center aisle. She came in early. I greeted her and introduced myself.

She promptly told me her Katrina story. She lived for years in the Lakeview neighborhood where our church is located. The flood destroyed her home. She permanently relocated to a small town in central Louisiana. A faith community there reached out to her, and she now attends every Sunday. She came to our church during a visit to New Orleans because she said she wanted to thank God for the journey of faith the flood caused her to travel.

Shortly thereafter, a couple I had not seen before slipped into a pew. They informed me they had evacuated in Hurricane Katrina and were only now, almost ten years later, returning permanently to our city.

Week by week—almost day by day—without prompting or questioning, I hear the Katrina stories. I tell my own story often in response to the queries of strangers. The evacuation on the contraflow, the destruction of my daughters' homes, the church facility as a relief center, our deployment of 21,000 volunteers, building 91 homes in partnership with Habitat, gutting more than 1,000 flooded homes—these are components of my own narrative.

A Baptist denominational executive from Texas said he was surprised and delighted to see the diversity in the membership of First Baptist New Orleans after his recent visit to our church.

We are black and white, Asian and Latino, and all over the economic scale as a church. This diversity is in part the legacy of Hurricane Katrina.

The devastation of Hurricane Katrina forced an outward focus for our church. Clean up and rebuilding programs, educational ministries, feeding initiatives, medical missions, and rehabilitation efforts involved hundreds of our members. I found myself working in Treme, Bywater, Mid-City, the Ninth Ward, Gentilly, East New Orleans, Chalmette, Lakeview, and virtually all over the flooded footprint of our city.

All the doors in the city stood ajar after the flood. There was little point in locking up. Everything was ruined. Driving down the streets you could see the debris line drawn by the floodwaters on every single structure, along with the gaping doors and windows on practically every house.

Those open doors were a vivid symbol to me of the new openness we all experienced in the crisis. Post-Katrina outreach connected our congregation with the wide range of people outside the doors of our church. As trust and friendships developed, a greater diversity of people gathered inside the building.

A permanent change occurred in the spirit and character of First Baptist New Orleans. Efforts to reach out to our neighbors continue unabated to this day. Authentic faith goes to the need and is not constrained by race or social standing.

Most importantly, Hurricane Katrina presented us with the opportunity to partner with Pastor Fred Luter and Franklin Avenue Baptist Church, a large and predominantly black congregation. Our two congregations shared education space, offices, and the worship center for more than two years. We joined forces to do men's, women's, and health ministries, prayer groups, summer camps, and fellowships of all kinds.

Our congregations learned to love each other deeply, and that bond of love remains strong a decade later. I was delighted to nominate Pastor Fred Luter to be the first black president of the Southern Baptist Convention. His candidacy was unopposed. The election occurred here in New Orleans on June 19, 2012. It was a moment of celebration for our churches and our convention that we will never forget.

Talking about race is not easy. Listening is even more difficult. Hurricane Katrina has given our city an unusual opportunity to set aside any prejudice and listen to the stories of others. We discover, if we listen, that our stories are similar, that we have the same dreams and we hold many concerns and priorities in common.

We rode the buses. We evacuated in helicopters. We got stuck on the contraflow. We were downtown in a vertical evacuation. We were at Baptist Hospital or the Superdome without working plumbing or electricity. We manned the boats and rescued the drowning and buried the dead.

Then we rebuilt our lives and community with the help of strangers and friends. We experienced the greatest deployment of volunteer support in American history, I expect, and we learned to appreciate the diversity and heart of this place that we call home.

God often speaks His most powerful word in the midst of the storm.

I have been hearing the Great Commandment ringing in my heart.

# PART TWO

# Neighbors' Needs

*A man was going down from Jerusalem to*

*Jericho, when he was attacked by robbers.*

*They stripped him of his clothes,*

*beat him and went away,*

*leaving him half dead.*

LUKE 10:30

## WHO DESERVES MY CARE?

S OMEONE WANTS TO TALK WITH YOU IN THE LOBBY," A DEACON told me, touching my arm. "Her name is Annie. I think she may be homeless."

You should stop for a moment and realize how common this interruption is for pastors everywhere. People who want assistance with food or fuel or housing often go to churches in and around their worship hours.

I was impatient with this stranger immediately. "Another emergency," I thought to myself, miserably, "and she wants me to solve it."

These encounters with needy travelers right after worship—they come too often.

I felt for my wallet in the back pocket of my suit pants. I had stopped carrying a wallet to church years ago. Too often it was empty when I got home. Today I had no wallet with me, no money on me. I was relieved. That's the truth.

*Who is Annie?* I wondered, pulling myself away from a pleasant conversation with friends in the center aisle of the sanctuary. I heaved a sigh and headed up the gradual incline toward the lobby. Most of the homeless are men—90 percent, I'd guess. A single homeless woman would be an anomaly. I wondered if she had a man with her who stayed outside and sent her in to get some cash.

Our post-Katrina world was filled with homeless people. Literally half of the congregation of First Baptist New Orleans lost their homes to the great flood. We were always a destination city for the traditional homeless population, and we always had our share of mentally ill and mentally challenged homeless living on our streets. Katrina had created a group we called "the new homeless"—people who were for the first time in their lives living on the streets because their houses were ruined. They included an unusual number of women and children.

A tent city had sprung up in the park next to City Hall. More than 300 homeless persons were living there without bathrooms or other accommodations. Well-meaning and concerned citizens and groups brought clothing and food to the park. We were among them. The park quickly became an eyesore, unsanitary and unsafe for its residents.

City officials were desperate for solutions. I talked to the mayor and suggested a way to increase the number of beds for the homeless. Obtaining proper construction permits from various agencies would slow down the project, I told him.

Our congregation pulled together a team of volunteers and built a structure on the grounds of New Orleans Mission that housed 120 men. City officials helped raise funds for the project and took care of all the permitting needs.

I care for the homeless. I was only 11 years old when I first encountered and reached out to the homeless. I sang for them, prayed with them, and ate with them at the rescue mission in El Paso under the instruction of my father. It's really where my ministry began.

But I was tired after months of storm recovery. I paused in the aisle as I approached the big wooden doors that entered the lobby. I took a moment, falling behind my escort. The needs were monumental. More than 100,000 homes in our city were flooded. Both of my own daughters lost their homes. We were perpetually hosting volunteer crews. It was never ending, or so it felt to me, and everybody needed something.

"Annie," I muttered under my breath. Usually people in need were nameless until they secured the pastor's attention. Then they did their introductions and told their stories.

The lobby of our sanctuary is expansive and impressive, a beautiful and bright space, filled with chatter after every worship service. It was bathed in sunshine as I entered it that day, and worshipers were still lingering, talking, and laughing. The deacon walked me over to Annie.

She stood straight with hands folded. Her back was toward the glass wall of the lobby. She was a small presence among those standing with her. Her clothes were an odd assortment, I noticed when I first laid eyes on her. Clothes are not something I usually notice. But hers were ill-fitting, baggy on her thin frame. She paid no attention when she put together that outfit, I thought.

I introduced myself, and she extended her hand to me. Her hand was small, even tiny, and I gripped it gingerly. She spoke softly with careful diction, slurred a little by weakness and weariness. She had a significant vocabulary, I noted, and she made eye contact when she addressed me.

I looked at her narrow face framed in shoulder-length, stringy blonde hair tinged with gray. Her skin was thin and taut on her face and arms. She had a small, sharp nose and a determined chin. She was older than I. The wrinkles around her eyes and neck gave away her age.

Her blue eyes had a sparkle, though. They danced a little. She was a feisty lady, I decided, with some grit and fight left in her despite the hard times.

I assumed many things about Annie before I ever met her. Some of those things were true. She did have an emergency. She was homeless. Other assumptions proved untrue. She had no male companion waiting for her in the car. She was not trying to transfer her problem to me.

We can develop a cynicism about people in need. We might assume when we see them that they are weak and sick because they have not been disciplined in their eating or exercising or personal habits. We might assume that they are homeless because they are lazy, unwilling to work. We might assume that they are broke because they cannot hold a job. We might assume that they need clothes and food because they are slothful and have a drug or alcohol problem.

We are like the disciples who, coming upon a blind man, immediately ask Jesus, "Rabbi, who sinned, this man or his parents, that he was born blind?" (John 9:2). They automatically connected his blindness from birth to moral failure, either his own or that of his parents.

Jesus corrected their ignorance. "'Neither this man nor his parents sinned,' said Jesus, 'but this happened so that the works of God might be displayed in him'" (John 9:3). In a way, Jesus was saying that it was not the moral failure of the sick person, but it was the moral question before the observer that was at issue. "The works of God might be displayed in him" points not to something that the blind man might do but to the work that Jesus was about to do, or one of His disciples, perhaps.

This is the moral quandary we experience when we confront need in another human being. We feel the desire to help, to do something. We realize that God might use us to do His work in and through the need.

Cynicism is the end result of saying to ourselves, "That's not my problem. That's his problem. That's his parents' problem."

"Where is his family?" we wonder. "Why doesn't this person do something?" We feel that the individual himself—and perhaps his family—is responsible for the problem and therefore responsible to fix it.

What if we saw human need as the opportunity to display the works of God rather than seeing human need as a display of the failures of a person? What if God's glory is displayed in the addressing of human need even more so than the pilgrimage to His house of worship? Isn't all human need—physical, emotional, or spiritual—an opportunity for such display?

> *But God chose the foolish things of the world to shame the wise; God chose the weak things of the world to shame the strong. God chose the lowly things of this world and the despised things—and the things that are not—to nullify the things that are, so that no one may boast before him.*
>
> —1 CORINTHIANS 1:27–29

If we listen to Jesus we will hear that the cause and effect of human need is the display of God's glory. We should not attempt to soften or nuance the perspective of Jesus expressed in this passage. Rather, we should receive the full force of it in our minds and hearts. Human need is present before us in order that the works of God may be displayed. If this viewpoint prevails in our hearts it will keep us from cynicism, inaction, and despair in the face of human need. Seeking to discover the work that brings God glory should be the first movement of our hearts in the presence of such need.

Annie showed up more than once. She never gave us her last name. Someone called her "Raggedy Annie," and with that moniker from

Johnny Gruelle's fictitious orphan, we distinguished her from all the other Annies in our world.

Annie was a bottomless pit of endless need, nearly helpless in a personal world turned upside down by the great flood.

She surprised all of us, as it turned out, and enriched our lives as we provided for her what she could not do for herself.

## WHO ARE THESE PEOPLE IN NEED?

It's a common story. People are often in need. I will be more needy in the future than I am today.

I feel the stubble on my chin as I awake in the morning. My lips may be pursed as if I am toothless. My back is often hurting from walking 18 holes of golf or working in the yard—dragging limbs and hacking away at weeds around the house. I am aware most mornings of my own inexorable march toward the weakened condition of old age.

I predict that one day you will need others to care for you. You will want their care to be loving and kind, provided in a way that preserves your dignity.

I predict that very soon someone will need you to care for them. They will want that care to be loving and kind, provided with dignity.

None of us should be surprised by weakness and illness either in ourselves or in those we love. We are all moving into a future full of needs. This may be the most predictable truth about our future.

Now would be a good time to shed the cynicism about the weak and the sick. Now would be a good time to drop the denial. We and our loved ones are all aging. None of us is immortal.

We are all Annie, and we are all Annie's helpers at some time or other.

I knew she was God's assignment for us, our neighbor in need, when I first laid eyes on her. This is true despite my sour attitude at the moment I met her. I had been preaching and teaching on the truth that God selects our neighbors for us. I was impressed by the Spirit when I saw Annie that she was my neighbor, even if she was a nuisance to me.

She was dressed in those secondhand garments. She needed a place to stay for the night.

We called the New Orleans Mission, and they told us that Annie had exceeded her permitted stays, but that they would provide again for her that night. She drove out of the parking lot in a beat-up sedan with boxes, clothes, and blankets in all the vacant seats, and I could see she had been living in her car.

Annie returned repeatedly to worship with us and sometimes had evident needs. We put her up at a nearby hotel. She attended a Sunday School class and was warmly received. People connected to her—an articulate and charming elderly lady.

We learned she suffered from post-surgical pain in her side, and we asked how we might help her. She surprised us all by telling us that she needed help cleaning up her place in Lakeview, the neighborhood where our church facility is located. "Annie has a home?" we all thought to ourselves. She had received a notice from the code enforcement officer, she said. We were quite familiar with that problem in our post-Katrina devastation. "Who is this woman?" we all wondered. We still didn't even know her last name.

A crew of volunteers from our church arrived at her four-plex apartment building. It was flooded in Katrina and subsequently gutted. It was all bare studs with no finished surfaces, no working appliances, and no utility service. Not even running water. We learned that Annie was living and working out of an upstairs apartment when the heat and cold were not too severe. We cleaned up her yard but knew that we were not addressing Annie's real need.

Numerous church members were drawn into the orbit of Annie's needs. We worked with her to find a suitable and permanent home, driving her around town from one address to another. She finally settled upon an apartment in Mid-City, and we arranged for a moving day.

Annie stumbled and fell in the church aisle one Sunday. A physician present for worship helped her. The next time she had an appointment with her doctor, my assistant, Madelyn, accompanied her. We learned that Annie had colon cancer and that her condition was terminal.

The moving crews arrived at her upstairs apartment to sort through the mounds of papers, gather and wash the stacks of old clothes (12 loads), and transport her meager belongings to her new address. They returned to the church with several large political signs: "Anne Thompson for Governor."

Annie was indeed a Louisiana gubernatorial candidate in 1991 and 1995 and ran for the U.S. Congress in 1992. She was a Phi Beta Kappa award recipient and earned a Ph.D. in Spanish from Tulane University. Annie taught at various colleges and universities during her distinguished academic career.

Hurricane Katrina flooded both of her properties in Lakeview. Before she could restore them, she fell under the pale of her sickness. She failed to comprehend her true condition. She wanted to return to a life that was forever lost to her. She became one of the thousands of newly homeless people in our city.

We moved Anne Thompson and her meager belongings into an apartment on Saint John Bayou near our church. Annie died with dignity in her own apartment, lying next to a window that overlooked a cemetery and the fairgrounds. She had peace with God, she said, but she did not want to die. She loved life, and she was leaving too many unfinished tasks.

We conducted a memorial service at our church. Many of those drawn into the orbit of her need were there. A few of her friends who had lost track of her in the post-Katrina chaos heard of her passing and joined us for the service.

Many friends and even family members, out of touch since Katrina, learned of Annie's circumstances only when her obituary was published. Fond remembrances were shared by a small group of former colleagues and new acquaintances in a memorial service at First Baptist New Orleans.

No government agency or statistics will confirm this, but Anne Thompson was a victim of Hurricane Katrina. Elderly and sick, she could not pull together her life dismantled by the great storm.

Annie's story is only one of thousands among the displaced population of our city. She reminds us that the down-and-out are people just like us. One day they may be us. We cannot dismiss them with our stereotypes. We will never live abundantly if we take that course.

We will not forget Raggedy Annie. We are blessed that she appeared in our church lobby that day, needing a bed for the night. She reminds us of the great opportunity human need affords us to demonstrate the love of neighbor and bring glory to the Father in Heaven. And she reminds us that the stereotypes with which we dismiss those in need are really just excuses we use to escape our responsibility. What we actually forfeit in turning our back on human need is the hand of God upon our lives.

## IDENTIFYING MY NEIGHBOR

The expert in the law has a question for Jesus: "Who is my neighbor?" His first question was, "What must I do to inherit eternal life?" Jesus threw that one back at him, and the expert in the law answered his own question by saying that the two great commandments are to love God and love neighbor. Jesus tells him this is correct. But he wants to justify himself because he is not sure that he is keeping the second commandment. So he asks about the definition of "neighbor." This prompts Jesus to tell the story of the Good Samaritan (see Luke 10:25–37).

### YOUR NEIGHBOR IS NOT SIMPLY
### THE PERSON NEXT DOOR

How broad is the term "neighbor" in the second commandment? We generally use the term "neighbor" to refer to those who live near us geographically. The Bible uses the term in this same way, as illustrated in the instructions about the eating of the Passover meal in Exodus 12:4. If the meal is too large they should share it with their "nearest neighbor."

The tenth commandment in the Decalogue (the Ten Commandments) is a companion to this second commandment: "You shall not covet your neighbor's wife. You shall not set your desire on your neighbor's house or land, his male or female servant, his ox or donkey, or anything that belongs to your neighbor" (Deuteronomy 5:21). The neighbor referred to here would undoubtedly encompass more than the person next door. It would not be right to covet *anyone's* wife or possessions. Coveting is excluded for the people of God.

So who is my neighbor? Jesus tells the story of the Good Samaritan to answer this specific question, but He does not give an address for one's neighbor. He does not locate the parable in a neighborhood but on the roadside between two cities. By so doing, He is identifying our neighbors.

The parable concerns people who are traveling from Jerusalem to Jericho and seem to have no prior association. According to Jesus, no further explanation about geography or relationship is necessary to identify the neighbor.

We do not know where the victim is from. We do not know his ethnicity or religion. We only know that he is traveling between Jerusalem and Jericho.

We do not know where the Samaritan lives—only that he is a Samaritan traveling this road. He is probably not from Jericho because he does not take the man home—he puts him up in an inn.

## YOUR NEIGHBOR IS NOT NECESSARILY A PERSON OF YOUR ETHNICITY OR CULTURE

The expert is looking for two players in the story that Jesus tells. He is looking for himself, and he is looking for his neighbor. We do this when we hear stories. We identify with the characters in it. We look for ourselves in timeless tales.

Jesus mentions robbers. The expert says to himself, "That doesn't sound like me." He mentions the priest, and the expert may expect that this is his character. But when the priest moves to the other side of the road and walks by the wounded man, the expert probably concludes that this priest is not his character in the story. The expert's interest was piqued by mention of a Levite, but the Levite hurries away from the wounded man just as the priest did, walking by on the other side of the road. The Levite is not the hero in the story. He is obviously not the one who demonstrates love of neighbor. So the expert in the law is still looking for his character in the story.

Then comes the Samaritan. The Jews despised these half-breeds. They had married non-Jews and mixed with the people of the land. They developed their own culture and customs and even religion. No good Jew could identify with a Samaritan in any story.

The expert in the law is now groping for his place. Who is he in this tale? He is no Samaritan. Therefore, he is forced in his mind to be the man in the ditch. He could easily be a victim of robbers on his own trip from Jerusalem to Jericho.

The expert who asked the question, "Who is my neighbor?" must now identify, not with the hero, but with the victim in the story.

Jesus makes ethnicity an issue. He "plays the race card," as we would say in New Orleans and elsewhere. Jesus could certainly have told the story without mentioning race or ethnicity. He chose not only to mention it but to make it a centerpiece of the parable, a distinguishing mark of his answer to the question about neighbors. A person of any race or nationality can be my neighbor and can be a neighbor to me.

Barriers and boundaries are a universal reality for humans. No matter what place or what time you live in, you are confronted with the challenge of who to love and how to love them. Ethnicity tends to separate us. It may be harder for us to identify with someone who is of a different ethnicity. But this difference is superficial, even artificial. People of any ethnicity are worthy of respect.

You may argue that a Samaritan is a half-Jew and therefore more likely to be embraced by a Jew than, say, a Gentile. In fact, it may puzzle you that Jesus chooses a Samaritan over a Gentile to illustrate that ethnicity is not a factor.

Nothing divides the human family so deeply as small differences. This is easy to illustrate from the world of religion. Wes Jackson, a colleague and former religion editor for *The Times-Picayune* in New Orleans, made the observation one day that small differences divide denominations. This was his viewpoint as a long-tenured religion editor and one not particularly committed to any religion.

It's not that the differences we have as families are insignificant. But it is that they loom much larger in our own minds than they do to outsiders. In fact, the theological nuances that frequently divide Baptists are a complete mystery to many outside observers.

So it is with ethnicity. The *proximity* of our second cousins is part of the problem. Geographically, Samaritans share borders with Jews. Ethnically, Samaritans share lineage with Jews. Religiously, Samaritans share the Old Testament with Jews.

*Purity* is another part of the problem. Those who believe they have the pure truth are always enraged at those who pollute that truth with a mixture of what appears to be falsehood to them. We tend to condemn, not those who are our opposites, but those who are our offending counterparts.

And a large part of it is *pride*—pride in who I am and what I have achieved, in my heritage and culture. I grow up suspecting that I am part of the greatest family in the greatest nation in the greatest generation. This is true for me whether I live in the slums of Rio de Janeiro or the condominiums of Manhattan. So do we elevate our own importance.

The expert in the law is a Jew. Jesus could have had a Jew helping a Samaritan. In that case, the benevolent Jew would have been the hero of the story. Instead, he had a benevolent Samaritan helping someone we assume to be a Jew. The expert in the law is almost forced by the story to the role of victim. He would not want to identify with either the priest or the Levite. He would most naturally identify with the hero. But since the hero turns out to be a Samaritan, the expert is most likely to identify with the man in the ditch.

Jesus reverses these roles to be even more emphatic about the universal truth that all men are created equal. A Samaritan is as deserving as a Jew to play the lead role. If this is true, then it goes without saying that a Samaritan is as deserving as a Jew to be the one who is rescued.

Jesus does not cast the Jewish expert in the hero's role. Instead, he is the victim. In this way, He teaches not that Jews should be kind to

Samaritans but that Samaritans have full dignity and worth and are able to be heroes in the work of love, the work of God. We must hear this truth again and again before it settles in our hearts.

## YOUR NEIGHBOR MAY BE ECONOMICALLY DISADVANTAGED

This victim, by all appearances, is broke. He has not a dime to his name. Maybe somewhere in some distant state or city he has two coins to rub together, but not here between Jerusalem and Jericho. And for our hero, any distant wealth is irrelevant. He assumes that the victim cannot help himself, that he has no access to resources even for lodging.

Jesus has a man with a donkey doing the helping. He is also a man with oil and wine on his person. And he is a man with coins in his pocket. This Samaritan would be considered pretty well off by some in his day.

We are more separated by economic standing than by any other factor, including race. The church must reach out to all people, no matter their material prosperity. In this case, a man with means helped a man whose money was dishonestly taken from him.

Jesus had a unique ability to relate to people of all economic levels, from Zacchaeus and Joseph of Arimathea to the lepers, the widows, and the blind beggars. He was able to do this because He sustained an amazing freedom from the tyranny of money.

These categories appear not to matter in identifying your neighbor: address, race, and economic standing. A person may be a neighbor to me and me to him regardless of color or occupation.

The question is, "Who is my neighbor?"

The answer is, "The Samaritan is a neighbor."

Now how can that be an answer to the question?

It is an answer because if the Samaritan is a neighbor to the victim, then the victim is also a neighbor to the Samaritan. If the man next door is a neighbor to me, then I am a neighbor to him. It is a reciprocal relationship.

## TWO THINGS MATTER IN IDENTIFYING YOUR NEIGHBOR

1. Need Matters: "The one who had mercy on him"

> *If anyone has material possessions and sees a brother or sister in need but has no pity on him, how can the love of God be in that person? Dear children, let us not love with words or speech but with actions and in truth.*
>
> —1 JOHN 3:17–18

A neighbor is someone in need. We all have needs. Sometimes those needs become apparent to those around us. When they do, and someone steps in to help us, we experience the interaction of the second commandment.

From this time forward, any Samaritan in need will certainly be a neighbor to the expert in the law. Previously, perhaps, he had defined "neighbor" as "blood brother" or "kin" or "someone like me." Now he knows better. If I *can* be a neighbor to someone, then that someone *is* my neighbor.

2. Opportunity Matters: "Go and do likewise"

> *If anyone, then, knows the good they ought to do and doesn't do it, it is sin for them.*
>
> —JAMES 4:17

Much about the story of the Good Samaritan is spatial and temporal in nature. It happens at a certain place. It happens at a certain time. Had any of the four key players taken another route, the scene would have played out differently. The priest or Levite would have been absolved of his guilt. The victim would not have been victimized. Or the Samaritan would not have been obliged and inconvenienced.

Much of it is "chance" or "happenstance." The priest "happened to be going down the same road." The King James Version translates, "And by chance there came down a certain priest thatway" (Luke 10:31). The circumstances afforded the opportunity both for neglect and for compassion.

We do not choose our neighbors. They are chosen for us by chance and happenstance—by providence, no less. The priest might have lamented that he was put in such an uncomfortable position. Had he gone another way, he would not have had to choose. The same is true for the Levite and the Samaritan. Our desire to inherit eternal life is dependent upon Providence and His grace. So also is our opportunity to care for the stranger.

We choose, not the place or the time, but our response to the evident need. My neighbor is one to whom I can be a neighbor.

We need to be careful that we do not underestimate our ability to help. We have a great capacity to care for those around us. We have the ability, not only to help individuals in need, but also to help with the systemic problems that wound and debilitate our neighbors.

The identity of your neighbor, whom you are to love, is no mystery at all. In the course of your day, you will pass him by. He is someone in need, and he is someone that you can help.

Residents of New Orleans and the Gulf Coast have vivid memories of Hurricane Katrina and its aftermath. We remember the Good Samaritan spirit that seems to overtake all of us in emergencies and catastrophes. Strangers helped strangers. People rescued one another. Ordinary activities suspended out of necessity because we could no longer go merrily on our way to work or the gym. So we turned aside to help each other. We exercised a concern for each other that is admirable and unusual. Many of us were the recipients of amazing love from strangers during our weeks and months of continued evacuation.

The man in the ditch is an unfortunate victim of robbers. In some ways, it is a catastrophe of one, a solitary disaster. As such, it is much more common than the great flood of New Orleans. These solitary dramas of destruction and death work their way out every day around us. But they are not on a scale that causes the necessary suspension of other activities.

The Samaritan recognizes the unfolding disaster with one casualty. He turns aside from his busy day to help the man in need. He does not need a paralyzing natural disaster or national crisis to know that this is his opportunity and duty under God.

And we must learn this truth. We are way too comfortable with the daily march of corruption, violence, and poverty. We must not wait for the storm. Our waiting is sin. There is much that we can do in the here and now, with circumstances as they are, to keep the first and second commandments. These are not optional for us. They are not to be kept only "if we have time" or if normal activities are suspended.

We must learn to live and obey the second commandment as a daily part of our lives. It is essential for our gospel proclamation. Keeping the second commandment is the only thing that makes our words believable.

## REFLECTIONS

1. Why did Jesus introduce the issue of race in answering the question, "Who is my neighbor?"
2. What does this race issue stir up in you?
3. Would you be willing to let God select your neighbor for you?

## FINDING NEIGHBORS WITH NEEDS

A couple who were new to the church came to my office to tell me what was going on in their lives. The wife told a story about leaving church one Sunday—we gather to go to the need, you know—determined to reach out to a neighbor with the love of Christ. She did not know who, though.

She "adopted" a stranger, an elderly lady residing in a nursing home nearby. She told me that for months she had made weekly visits to the nursing home. She developed a friendship with the resident. She took her shopping and provided for her in many other ways.

Finding that neighbor in need was not a long process for her. It was as simple as driving down the street to a residential facility and striking up a conversation.

I fielded a call one day from someone in Texas who heard about the diversity of ministries we operate in our city. Poverty in Orleans Parish, where our church is located, stands at 29 percent of the population. We minister amidst a cacophony of evident needs. The caller wanted to know if I had any ideas about what she and others could do in a rural setting.

The church in the rural setting has often been a stabilizing force amidst changing population demographics. It is the depository of our cherished values. Among our social institutions, the rural church often stands out as the place that feels most safe and familiar to us. It may represent in our minds how things ought to be and, maybe, used to be.

I was pastor to several rural churches through the years, and I maintain loving relationships with a number of congregations that I visit when I can. Some of my mentors in the faith are stalwarts in these beloved churches.

Rural churches are often on the front lines in taking the gospel and the love of Christ to persons in need. In fact, any congregation or Christian who desires to follow Christ in the ministry to hurting people may do so right where they live.

Our neighbors who live in poverty really need good news. They live with a complex mix of challenges that may include illiteracy and low education levels in general, limited access to health care, unemployment and under-employment, family disintegration, immigration issues, and housing and transportation needs. High incidents of crime and drug use may also plague their families and communities. In other words, if you live near pockets of poverty, you may be able to show God's love and share good news in a variety of settings. You can assess something of your local situation by taking a look at "Mapping Poverty in America" as published in the *New York Times*, January 4, 2014.

Our neighbors in need often reside in institutions in our communities. Make sure that you cooperate by conforming your ministry to the guidelines and protocols of the institutions you enter. You want to be a good neighbor, not a nuisance. You are on their turf, and they may have different priorities than you have. Many staff members see their occupation as a way to care for others. Treat both staff and residents as neighbors to love.

I was standing on the playground beside an assistant principal one afternoon at John Dibert Community School, a public school near our church facility. We were watching our church volunteers as they set up a fair for the Dibert students and families. He said, "This is something I have never seen before—an actual volunteer!" Community schools are great places to give volunteer hours and find ways to help. They will also help you understand the larger picture of needs in your community. Make a visit and talk to the principal and/or social worker.

You will not find a population more open to your loving concern than those incarcerated in your local jail or prison. Get in touch with law enforcement officials and find out what process is required to become a regular volunteer. Remember the words of Jesus, "I was in prison and you came to visit me" (Matthew 25:36). Also, remember that correctional officers must focus on security as their first priority. Follow all the rules of the institution, or you may not be invited to return!

Institutions for assisted living and independent living as well as convalescent and nursing homes are important places for followers of Jesus to be at work. This is a traditional setting of ministry for our churches and one that we should never neglect.

Hospitals are great places to reach out with the love of God. Ramp up the care for your own church members when they are in the hospital, and you will continually meet new people—staff, patients, and family members—to whom you can minister.

Missions, transitional housing facilities, and rehabilitation centers usually welcome and solicit the involvement of volunteers. Opportunities abound to help those who have fallen by the wayside.

I will never forget the moment I learned the true vulnerability of undocumented residents in our communities. I was trying to persuade a gunshot victim, still bleeding from the wound, to ride with me to the emergency room of a local hospital. He refused to get in the car. I had already experienced this same situation previously with a stabbing victim and a rape victim with contusions and broken ribs. *What is wrong with these people?* I thought. *Why won't they go to the hospital?* I thought that they could access our health care without revealing their immigration status or getting involved with law enforcement officers.

I was wrong. If it appears that they have been hurt in the commission of a crime, medical personnel are required to call law enforcement officials.

So undocumented residents of your community are likely the most victimized people that you will meet. They will not call the police, and, if criminals rob, rape, or shoot them, they will not go to the hospital. They are easy targets for thieves and thugs and unscrupulous business owners. They live in the shadows, performing the most menial tasks for us, without access to these basic provisions that we take for granted.

As a general rule, the most vulnerable people in town are those who recently arrived. They do not know the community, and they have few friends. International students and immigrants often need our love and support upon arrival. As I write this I am thinking about Hansi. She came to see me last Sunday, moved to tears as she trusted in Christ and presented herself for baptism. We first met her through a ministry to international students.

Loving these strangers will definitely connect you to the heart of Christ and to the ancient context of "love your neighbor as yourself" (Leviticus 19:18). Many new arrivals may struggle with the language. Teaching English as a Second Language (ESL) may be a great opportunity to get to know them and share the love of Christ. Our ESL ministry at FBNO has connected us in significant ways to people of other faiths and cultures.

Every culture in every generation struggles with the opportunities and problems of immigration, legal and illegal. This includes the fledgling nation of Israel as they sought to establish themselves in their Promised Land. What do we do with these foreigners and strangers among us?

We have been given the answer to this question repeatedly in the inspired text. We love them, of course. This command and call of Christ could not be more explicit.

Our role as caregivers, not law enforcement, is evident in another ministry that may or may not be an opportunity in your community. We reach out to the employees of clubs on Bourbon Street. The dancers, in particular, need our encouragement and love. We send women, not men, into the strip joints. They keep their eyes on faces and try not to let their gaze wander. We have experienced the joy of seeing young ladies, runaways from their homes, reunited with parents. We help them find jobs where they can also find dignity and security. Some of the dancers and bouncers have reached out to us as we leave emergency numbers for them to call. Some have attended our church.

Reaching out to those in the sex industry may sound strange, but to us it definitely feels like Jesus' work. Remember that prostitute who washed His feet? Remember when He told the Bible teachers, "The tax collectors and the prostitutes are entering the kingdom of God ahead of you" (Matthew 21:31)?

Sometimes Jesus just drives me crazy.

## THE STRUGGLE TO UNDERSTAND POVERTY

The entire Florida Housing Community, home to thousands in the Upper Ninth Ward of New Orleans, flooded when the levees broke. The brightly colored multi-family units, constructed just prior to the storm, were boarded up after the flood and stood empty for years in a meadow of hip-high grass and weeds.

Our church ministry team began to discuss in the fall of 2004, prior to the flood, how we could take our "Florida" ministry to the next level and what that level might be. We started two churches in the area in the previous 14 years and helped with recreation, tutoring, food, health care, legal services, Vacation Bible Schools, revivals, evangelism, and discipleship.

We did not know what to do next, but we knew that what we were doing was not enough. We taught Scripture and demonstrated the love of Christ, but we hadn't changed the economic and social forces that ensnared this community in the cycle of poverty. We longed to make a permanent difference in the future of these families.

I gave many tours of the Upper Ninth Ward trying to explain to people the conditions that existed even before Hurricane Katrina and the reasons for our effort to provide affordable, safe, and decent housing for these families.

Not everyone is sympathetic.

Many saw the post-Katrina pictures of chaos and confusion, the dead and the dying, and their hearts were moved with compassion.

Still others watched New Orleans in the wake of the storm and wondered why "those people" lived in such poverty. Some responded with shock and compassion. Others responded with confusion and disbelief.

I do not understand all the social forces that propagate poverty, ignorance, and violence. But, I have tried to be a careful listener and observer during my years in New Orleans as a reporter and as a pastor. I attend many community meetings in the inner city where I listen, with astonishment, to the point of view of those who have lived all their lives in poverty and among the poor. I cannot "get in their skin," but I have learned through the years to appreciate more fully the great difficulty of their situation.

I remember the moment I learned that the valedictorian of a high school senior class in New Orleans could not graduate because she failed the State of Louisiana standardized tests that are mandated for graduation.

The New Orleans Baptist Association established a medical clinic in the Ninth Ward in part because the life expectancy in the Lower Ninth Ward is currently 25 years less than the life expectancy in the neighborhood five miles away where our church is located.

A cycle of poverty exists in New Orleans in part because the disadvantaged who live in our community do not receive the same levels of education, protection, nutrition, shelter, and medical attention that other Americans receive. Those trapped in poverty are mostly women and children.

## REFLECTIONS

1. How would you evaluate your existing compassion ministries?
2. What criteria would you use to assess such ministries?
3. How could your church increase the impact of your good work?

## ROUTINE CARE OF MEMBERS

The new command is "love one another" (John 13:34). Jesus wants His disciples to care for each other deeply.

Many deeds of compassion are worked into the fabric of church life. These good works bear abundant and surprising fruit, and they should be nurtured and expanded. These include contacting guests who attend worship or small groups, calling those who are sick or absent, and visiting those who are bereaved or in the hospital. Texting, writing cards, sending emails, and leaving phone messages are some of the ways we routinely express care for others. Jesus said even a cup of cold water comes with a reward (Matthew 10:42).

Every Sunday we solicit information about the needs of our church members. We urge them to communicate with us through an "info tab" on each worship guide. These needs are summarized in a prayer report that is emailed and updated daily. The list includes all members in nursing homes and in hospitals. It also includes any scheduled medical procedures of which we are aware. Ministers and deacons make visits and file updated information with our office manager.

Small groups are the primary vehicle for delivery of care to church members in most congregations, including our own. Belonging to a small group is of utmost importance. Every small group should regularly assess its own infrastructure, making sure that loving care is given to its members in need. Daily prayer reports and prayer requests should be routine for small groups. Meal trains can be organized when such care is appropriate. At FBNO, we call this loving activity "community care," referring to the faith community and its internal caregiving.

We deliver hot meals every Wednesday evening to those who are sick, homebound, or just gave birth. These meal deliveries have become a regular part of our strategy of care.

We are blessed to have resources for financial care of the congregation. This enables us to contact members who may be struggling financially and provide for them in their time of need.

Our deacons care for widows in our congregation in special ways. This is part of their regular assignment.

Caregiving does not become routine until it is in the job description of an ongoing part of the community of faith. It must also be on the calendar and in the budget of our church.

## CREATING EASY ACCESS TO NEIGHBORS IN NEED

First Baptist New Orleans was embraced by people from all over the world in the aftermath of Hurricane Katrina. Literally thousands of people came to us wanting to help. We organized and deployed these volunteers into the flood zone. Those clean-up and recovery efforts shaped the personality and mission of our church in a specific and unusual way.

The recovery from the great flood is still ongoing. But after two or three years, church life had to return to some semblance of normalcy. We settled into a new normal as a city and a congregation. The new normal for our church was a heightened sense of the need and a new level of involvement in our community.

Our church staff was in a brain-storming session. Anna Palmer, minister of missions at the time, scribbled colorful notes on all the windows in her office. We were working on the integration of compassion ministries into the weekly schedule of our church. We wanted to make ministry to neighbors in need as readily accessible to our members as we could possibly make it. We felt that if the orphans and widows and others in need were not on our church weekly calendar, then they would not be consistently on our hearts.

We wanted to make compassion ministries more integral to our DNA as a church.

Many things emerged out of that brain-storming session. We chose the name "Care Effect" as an umbrella term for the compassion ministries we envisioned. We then modified the Wednesday night schedule to scatter the congregation into the community rather than simply gather them within the church walls.

We envisioned Care Effect teams with individual leaders. We envisioned different levels of commitment from members based on the ministry demands. Ministries that required preparation such as Bible teaching would be at a different commitment level than ministries such as serving food that required only being present.

We did not know for sure how our ministries would be funded, though we could identify some funds that were available. But we knew that God was prompting this new effort to love our neighbors, and we knew that He would provide.

The Care Effect at First Baptist New Orleans was first organized and implemented in 2008 by Anna. Along with Bob Moore, associate pastor and minister of pastoral care, and Christi Gibson, our minister of connections, Anna designed Care Effect to include three movements: City Care, Community Care, and Connecting Care. City Care is the spectrum of ministries beyond our own walls as a church. Community Care and Connecting Care implement our care for one another in the community of faith. The same impulse of the heart that motivates us to deliver a hot meal to a homebound person also motivates us to carry God's love to a juvenile offender.

The bulk of our Care Effect ministries are to those outside our own church family. Every week volunteer teams operate these ministries:

FEEDING STATIONS: We serve 300 hot meals each week. The food is delicious and is prepared by Virginia Johnson, a church member and restaurateur, at her catering facilities. Designated members of the two feeding teams pick up the food in hot boxes at the restaurant and carry them to the feeding stations. Each feeding team has about ten members. They serve the food outdoors. Team members always spend time talking to and praying with those who come. Through the years, relationships have been developed and ministry has expanded beyond the feeding station. Anyone can show up on Wednesday evening and help.

FUEL THE FUTURE, FEED A CHILD: This ministry is a response to the high level of child hunger in Louisiana and New Orleans, the highest in the nation, and is a cooperative venture with five public schools in our city. Church members add "kid-friendly" items to their regular shopping lists and bring these items to church. Volunteers pack them into backpacks that are carried to the schools on Thursdays. Principals, teachers, and social workers identify the children who are most at risk of hunger over the weekends. They send the children home on Friday afternoon with a backpack full of food for the weekend. Currently, five other churches partner with us in various ways to accomplish this good work.

Buying food, especially child-friendly packaging, is expensive. We are grateful for World Hunger funds provided through the North American Mission Board and the Louisiana Baptist Convention who are significant partners in our feeding ministries.

ENGLISH AS A SECOND LANGUAGE (ESL): We offer two semesters each year of ESL for recent immigrants. Volunteers in this ministry must receive training and make a semester-long commitment.

SUMMIT: Summit Kids Club is offered to 15–20 public school children from a school near our church facility. It is funded by the Fuel the Future Foundation, a nonprofit with an independent board, and seeks to help children at risk of failing achieve success in school and learn conflict management skills. Many of the children also participate in FBNO's regular children's ministries.

FOSTER CARE MINISTRY: In addition to Crossroads NOLA, a nonprofit organization that focuses on connecting children to families in foster care, FBNO offers a variety of support activities for foster families including respite care, date nights for foster parents, and the Foster Family Resource Center.

INWARD: This ministry is exclusively for women and reaches out to those who work on Bourbon Street and in other clubs in the city. Five churches partner with us in this ministry.

NURSING HOME OUTREACH: We conduct weekly worship in two nursing homes each Wednesday evening.

PRISON MINISTRIES: Volunteers conduct weekly Bible studies at the Orleans Parish Prison and at the Rivarde Juvenile Detention Center.

TUTORING MINISTRIES: Volunteers meet Sunday afternoons at the church to tutor children at risk of failing school.

RECREATION MINISTRIES: Volunteers conduct team sports for children and youth. This ministry is called Bunny Friend Ministry and is named after the city playground nearest Musicians' Village in the Upper Ninth Ward.

INTERNATIONAL CARE EFFECT: FBNO sends dozens of teams to Accra, Ghana, in West Africa, reaching out to a people group in that city who are largely without any gospel witness. Scholarships are available to make the trips possible for most church members who desire to go. A core part of the strategy is teaching ESL. A small group of believers have emerged through these years of witness.

Read more about the FBNO Care Effect ministries at fbno.org.

## CROSSROADS NOLA

Crossroads NOLA is a nonprofit organization led by Anna Palmer, previously our missions minister, with an independent board that receives grant money to recruit, train, and support foster families. Crossroads NOLA has 27 church partners, 30 families now certified for foster care, and 60 more families in the pipeline who have shown interest, made inquiries, and may continue the path toward certification.

The goal of Crossroads NOLA is to motivate churches to address the crisis in foster care in our region and our state. Many more foster families are needed if we are ever to treat these modern-day orphans with the love that Christ commands.

Crossroads NOLA provides curriculum and training for foster families and partners with the Louisiana Department of Child and Family Services (DCFS) in various ways.

The average foster family serves about 11 months. DCFS is the state agency that is charged with caring for children who are removed from their homes. It is severely underfunded in Louisiana and in many other states. This may explain in part why the outcomes for foster children are horrifying. More foster children end up in prison than graduate from college. Some 60 percent of prison inmates in Louisiana were in foster care as children.

Our church supports foster families in various ways. We occasionally underwrite special events at no cost for foster families. We maintain and operate the foster care resource center at our church facility. We provide "three-day bags" for DCFS to distribute. These bags are graded by age and sex and include everything the foster parent will need for three days for the child they receive. We also invested heavily in the renovation of a food truck that is now operating in partnership with District Donuts, a local restaurant that donates all profits from the food truck to Crossroads NOLA.

The foster children run up to me and give me hugs at church. They are precious to all of us. A number of the foster children have been formally adopted into families in our church. You can read all about Crossroads NOLA at crossroadsnola.org.

Supporting foster families is one way that almost every church can fulfill the biblical mandate to care for orphans. And when you see the foster children in your classes and choirs and on your church playground, you will be blessed.

## REFLECTIONS

1. Read James 1:27. What kind of religion does God accept as pure and faultless?
2. Do foster children qualify as modern-day orphans? Why or why not?
3. Would single mothers qualify as modern-day widows? Why or why not?
4. How could your church address the needs of foster children and families in your community?

# MID-WEEK CHURCH LOOKS DIFFERENT NOW

We have changed fundamentally the way we do church on Wednesday evenings. We scatter to the four winds. Some go east to the feeding station on Elysian Fields where we feed recent immigrants and others who live on the margins. Others go southeast to Bourbon Street to minister to employees in the clubs. Some go south to the Ozanam Inn (the Oz) where we feed those who are homeless or to the prisons to visit with inmates. Some go north to represent our church at the community fair or deliver meals to the homebound. Some go west to conduct worship at nursing homes.

Volunteer numbers surpassed 200 different individuals in just a few weeks after our launch of Care Effect in 2008. Through more than seven years of Care Effect, people of all ages have continued to show up at multiple sites in the inner city of New Orleans to feed the hungry, pray with the hurting, visit the sick, pass out gospel tracts, conduct Bible studies for juvenile offenders, and tutor school-age children.

Personal stories of transformation are told on both sides of Care Effect. The givers are receiving, and the receivers are giving. All in all, "it is more blessed to give than to receive," just as Jesus' words are recorded in Acts 20:35. People in the church are passionate about their ministries, connected to people in need, developing relationships, and feeling the spiritual exhilaration that only loving service provides.

Some teams stay at the church facility to teach ESL or tutor school children. Volunteers, including children and youth, also work in the Fuel the Future closet, a food pantry where we store the food and pack the backpacks. Almost every Wednesday, other projects are offered at the church facility in preparation for our Inward and Crossroads NOLA Care Effect teams.

Some of the projects require a semester-long commitment, such as tutoring children in the inner city or leading Bible study at the juvenile detention center. Other venues operate with a core of faithful volunteers supplemented weekly by those who help whenever they can come.

The church kitchen was already preparing meals for those in attendance at prayer meeting. Now we are also preparing meals for those recovering from surgery, sick at home, or just in need of a nutritious meal and some cheerful company. The "to-go" meals, delivered by volunteers, account for 20 percent of the meals prepared each Wednesday.

Mixing cool-aid or preaching a sermon—the range of tasks to be accomplished is wide. Anyone can plug in and find something useful and rewarding to do. Projects are added as needs arise. The ministries are in constant flux and continually evaluated. New ministries are contemplated to diversify tasks. Mothers and daughters, dads and their sons are serving together in ministries that translate the good news of Christ into practical deeds of kindness.

Some of us gather first for the fellowship meal. Many who come at that time are Summit Club kids and workers, ESL students and teachers, and Care Effect team members. We continue to offer a full schedule for youth and children each Wednesday evening, including involving them in their own work with Care Effect in various ways.

Music ministries continue each Wednesday evening along with prayer and Bible study.

Care Effect is the church *deployed* for mid-week worship on the go, out in the city, outside the four walls of the church. First Baptist New Orleans gathers on Sunday and scatters on Wednesday.

## REFLECTIONS

1. How do you balance love for one another with love of neighbors and strangers?
2. Is the care of orphans and widows in your personal schedule? Your church schedule?
3. How could the care of neighbors in need become more deeply embedded in your church DNA?

# WORKING TOGETHER

Church groups have considered New Orleans a destination of choice for many years. The North American Mission Board operates a variety of local inner-city ministries. Thousands of students arrive every spring break looking for ways to help. And thousands more come every summer to conduct recreation ministries, children's clubs, and every conceivable outreach to those at risk and in need.

As a pastor, I see these church groups come and go. Their numbers and energy amaze me. They work on projects of every description and are deployed through a host of local churches and ministries.

I know these volunteer groups make a difference in the lives of thousands of people. But I also know that they come and go like a water spout on the surface of Lake Pontchartrain. When the great volunteer influx of spring and summer is over, it is hard to tell what has been accomplished.

At various times before Hurricane Katrina, local church leaders talked about consolidating our efforts, putting a fine point on our purpose, and working together to achieve greater impact. That idea was met with interest and affirmation, but we had no central clearinghouse for projects or volunteers.

An administrative assistant at Baptist Community Ministries (BCM) called me in the fall of 2004. She asked if I could attend a meeting of a subcommittee of the board of directors. I told her I would be there.

BCM is the largest foundation in the state of Louisiana. It is focused on health care, law enforcement, and education in our city. But the board was anxious to join with other Baptist entities to expand their work and witness in New Orleans.

This question was put on the table by the board members of BCM for all of us to contemplate: "What can Baptists do together in our city?"

I leaned back in my chair. I knew what I was about to say was not common practice for Baptist churches. I knew that it fell outside of the BCM mission focus. But I also knew that I couldn't get it out of my heart.

I had attended a prayer breakfast for clergy hosted by then New Orleans Mayor Ray Nagin in the fall of 2004. The Mayor said something like this: "The single most important factor in lifting a family permanently out of poverty is home ownership." I borrowed a pen and wrote it down hastily. Even beyond education and job training, home ownership was the most important variable in bringing a family out of poverty into economic self-reliance.

"Let's build houses," I told the group at the BCM meeting. "Let's put together a building blitz and build an entire city block of homes."

"How many homes are you talking about?" a board member asked.

"I don't know," I replied. "I guess a city block would accommodate 40 homes, 10 on each side. We could establish a partnership with Habitat for Humanity."

"Would Habitat be able and willing to do that?" someone asked.

"I'll find out," I answered, and I felt a surge of hope and excitement in my soul. "If we did this together, it would be a great witness to our city. It would capture the imagination of our people. And it would change forever the economic future of 40 hardworking families in our city."

This idea, more than any other, energized the people in the meeting, and everyone left with a sense that we should launch further investigation and discussion.

I called the local chapter of Habitat and asked about a building blitz of 40 homes.

"We can do it," the local director said without the slightest hesitation. And so began the project that resulted in 91 homes being built in the Upper Ninth Ward to help lower-income families find a way out of poverty.

Building partnerships and coalitions is part of the future of compassion ministries in our churches. What we cannot do alone we are able to do together. Local associations may be able to help member churches join hands for the advance of the gospel through meeting needs in our communities. Cooperation puts a fine point on our efforts by harnessing the energy of many different individuals and groups to accomplish greater kingdom impact.

## REFLECTIONS

1. Is it acceptable for churches to partner with other entities to address human needs?
2. What parameters would you place on such a partnership?
3. Can you think of any groups who might become partners with you to address local needs?
4. Can you think of any groups now addressing community needs that might appreciate your help?

## WHAT DOES IT MEAN TO LOVE?

### LOVE TAKES A RISK

*He went to him.*

—LUKE 10:34

Love takes a risk. Love happens in a place and at a time. Love is more verb than noun.

We learn about love first from the poor example of the two religious authorities in this story of the Good Samaritan who got as far from the man as they could without inconveniencing themselves with a different route entirely.

The "other side of the road" is protection, a safe zone. It is where you go to keep on going where you want without putting yourself in jeopardy. By contrast, love will always put you at risk. No one knows this better than a woman giving birth.

The other side of the road is convenience, a buffer zone. The priest and the Levite passed by on the other side to prevent any detours or unexpected delays. No one knows better about inconvenience and delay than a mother caring for an infant. Love is always inconvenient.

Love takes a risk. Love notices and renders aid. Love walks into a trial. You never know what burden you will end up bearing when you decide to love.

Someone told me about the man who came upon a victim of crime in downtown New Orleans. Wanting to be a Good Samaritan, the man turned aside to help. He took the wounded man in his arms and called 911.

"I am here on Tchoupitoulas Street. A man is wounded and needs help," he told the operator.

"What street?" asked the 911 operator.

"Tchoupitoulas," he replied.

After a pause, the operator asked, "Could you spell that?"

The man thought for a moment and replied, "Give me five minutes. I'm going to drag him over to Canal."

When you turn aside to help someone in need, you may be asked to spell unusual names or attend unusual gatherings or go unusual places. Love always takes such risks.

Loving people in practical ways is extremely messy. You cannot sterilize the environment of the man in the ditch. You cannot remove all the dangers. You must simply step in and help.

God's people are very attached to their comforts, as are all people.

We shrink from danger. We often want to help, but we don't want to put ourselves or those we love at risk.

Love cannot operate without risk. Many people are called to come to New Orleans and help us. Some of them come to live here permanently. Sometimes parents or grandparents object to their moving to New Orleans. They want their children and grandchildren in a safer place.

Janet and I have friends who serve the Lord Jesus by spreading His Word and doing His deeds of love in many dangerous places. Often their wives and children accompany them to these distant places. The call of God is like that.

God loved us in this way: He sent His one and only Son to a dangerous place called Earth. He sent Him to a dangerous spot in the Middle East where heavily-armed soldiers patrolled the streets. He sent His only Son to a people ruled by a foreign power. He sent His Son knowing that He would be executed.

That is how God loved us. That is how love operates. That is how you will love. You will love by taking a risk.

## LOVE GETS INVOLVED

*He went to him and bandaged his wounds, pouring on oil and wine.*

—LUKE 10:34

Love gets involved. Love dresses the wounds and works for healing. Love is proximate—it is up close and personal.

Jesus puts no words for the wounded man in the Good Samaritan's mouth. The Good Samaritan never speaks to the wounded man in the parable.

Why? Because in this instance, words are not what is needed. The demand of love is not about a sermon. The demand of love is the supply of a very practical need. Love pours the healing vial.

Sometimes words are simply insufficient to express love. Pastor James wrote, "Suppose a brother or sister is without clothes and daily food. If one of you says to them, 'Go in peace; keep warm and well fed,' but does nothing about their physical needs, what good is it?" (James 2:15–16).

Our generation of believers in Jesus is quite enamored with words. In this way we are very much like the scribes who surrounded Jesus. We are like this expert in the law. He and his friends loved to sit around and discuss the meaning of "love your neighbor." They felt that they were pleasing God and doing God's work by having such discussions.

They focused on words, written and spoken. They reduced the commands of God to precise meanings. They thoroughly investigated the sacred texts. This was their preoccupation. They labored over these words, but they did not do the labor of practical deeds of kindness and love.

We often specialize in discussing words and their meanings. Too seldom do we get to the actual needs of the weary and wounded.

Love does not stop at pity. Loves shows compassion. "When he saw him, he took pity on him" (v. 33). He *took pity on him*. But he went beyond pity to action. Perhaps the religious authorities also had pity in their hearts for the poor man by the road. They might have muttered, "poor fellow," as they picked up their pace to get to their next appointment.

The Good Samaritan bandaged his wounds, pouring on oil and wine. Here we have the practical application of love. Love takes care of the immediate need. This man is loving his neighbor by giving him a bandage.

Love does whatever needs done.

The devastation of the island of Haiti by an earthquake spawned a verbal tsunami of religious speculation about cause and effect. Some blamed voodoo and some Catholicism for the ongoing crisis.

The same speculation followed Hurricane Katrina with the same dismal and misguided assessments about the faith and lifestyle of people in New Orleans. In each case, self-appointed prophets seemed compelled to pass judgment on the living, the dead, and the dying.

Religious leaders can grab a headline by pontificating on complex events that have no single or certain cause. The longing for meaning overcomes the obvious, and people fall prey to easy explanations for the troubles of others. When disaster becomes personal, however, the answers are not so easy to come by.

The Book of Job wrestles with the ancient spiritual question about why bad things happen to good people. Job is an exceptionally good man who experiences the collapse of family, wealth, and health from both man-made and natural causes. His main confession is this: "The LORD gave and the LORD has taken away; may the name of the LORD be praised" (Job 1:21). No one is completely good but God.

Sometimes goodness puts one at risk. Courageous and compassionate persons often choose to serve others in dangerous environs and die of disease and violence among those to whom they minister. Many earthquake victims in Haiti were just trying to help.

People of all faiths and no faith die in disasters. People of courage and good will can help with relief, restoration, and preventive measures. Explanations for disasters fall short, but responses to those disasters must be vigorous and ongoing. Most persons understand and embrace the moral obligation to help when others are in need.

Disasters often improve cooperation and discourse among populations partitioned by ideology, race, and religion. The devastation affords a new glimpse of the basics of living together on this planet. Catholics and Protestants develop bonds of friendship. Blacks and whites join forces. Republicans and Democrats work together. Immediate needs take priority over philosophical arguments.

The relatively small value of material possessions when compared with the value of friends and families becomes apparent after devastating earthquakes and floods. Material goods are once again assessed, not for their intrinsic worth, but for the value they possess in meeting human need.

One truth garners near-unanimous consent: whatever the cause, the call to help is compelling and far-reaching. When trouble comes—or when you meet it on the road—theologian and philosopher alike must rise from the chair and become boots on the ground.

## LOVE GOES THE SECOND MILE

*Then he put the man on his own donkey, brought him to an inn and took care of him.*

—LUKE 10:34

Love does not count the cost. Love pays the price. Love gives the donkey, takes care of the details, and discounts the delay.

Jesus knows exactly what it costs to stop in your busy schedule, use your own vehicle, and shell out the cash to help someone in need.

A donkey is a beast of burden, small and slow. Its pace is about that of a man walking, but it is able to bear significant burdens. If attached to a cart, a donkey can pull a considerable load. In many places in the world, donkeys are still used as a means of travel and transport of goods. The Good Samaritan used his donkey to help this wounded man. He suspended his own interests in favor of the injured man.

He traveled with him to the hotel. That is, he arranged his schedule so that he could travel with him.

He went back the next day to check on him and prepay for his expenses.

We read of the Good Samaritan's generosity, and we are amazed. He stops to help. He binds the wounds. He transports the man to the inn. He takes care of all expenses at the inn. Then he guarantees payment on an open-ended bill for anything that is required to care for the stranger.

Who lives like this? Who acts like this? Would you go this far in helping a stranger? Do you know anyone that would? Have we moved out of reality and into fantasy here?

I thought at first that we had—moved from reality to fantasy. When I truly thought about what this man did for the stranger, I could not envision myself, or anyone I knew, going this far.

And then I thought of what Jesus did for me. He did not pass me by. He stopped to render aid. He not only bound my wounds and took me to the inn, but He paid the ultimate price to rescue this poor sinner. He gave His life for me.

I do know a Good Samaritan who acts like this. His name is Jesus. And what He did for us, He now asks us to do for others. Having been loved with this kind of love, we are challenged to pass it on to our neighbors as well.

We will not out give God. When Jesus returns, He will repay us fully for all that we expend as the cost of loving our neighbors. "Look after him," said the Good Samaritan as he paid the bill. "When I return, I will reimburse you for any extra expenses you may have" (Luke 10:35).

I moved from feeling God's wrath and God's judgment in the wake of Hurricane Katrina to knowing that I was one of His favored ones, that I was the object of His grace rather than His anger. I made that journey in large measure because of the help that loving people gave to me and to all around me after the great flood.

The outpouring of love has that effect. It moves a wounded man from the ditch to the inn. It moves him in his spirit from a victim of evil to an object of love. This kind of self-giving, risk-taking, second-mile love is the most powerful force in the world. It transforms every environment where it is poured out. And it expresses most accurately the character of the God who sent His one and only Son to rescue us all.

## REFLECTIONS

1. Have you ever walked into a trial for the sake of love? Would you do it again?
2. How does the need shape the act of love that addresses it?
3. Are you content to love without any guarantee that the one you love will ever love you back?

# PART THREE

# Loving Deeds

*This happened so that the works of God*
*might be displayed in him.*

JOHN 9:3

## NEEDY ME

I AM NEEDY. I NEED FOOD. I NEED WATER. I NEED AIR.
I need protection from the elements. I need medical attention.

God has no needs. He is perfect and sufficient in Himself.

God's love does not address a need in His being, but my love does address a need. I need affection. I need to care for someone and have someone care for me. I am flesh and bone, body and blood, where God is not.

My love will always be touched by my need. This is why my giving is good for me. I receive something when I give out of the goodness of my heart, and I cannot help myself. I receive a deep sense of satisfaction when I give.

> *In everything I did, I showed you that by this kind of hard work we must help the weak, remembering the words the Lord Jesus himself said: "It is more blessed to give than to receive."*
>
> —QUOTED BY THE APOSTLE PAUL IN ACTS 20:35

You see my dilemma. I want to help the weak, the poor, and the needy. But I myself am weak, poor, and needy. I try to give away my hard-earned resources, but I keep getting back more than I can give. "My cup overflows" (Psalm 23:5).

All acts of loving sacrifice bless this needy me even more than the recipient. The needy one who is the object of my charity is not really the one who produces this return on my investment of love. Love in motion is its own reward. The blessedness is in the giving, not in the object of my gift.

My needy flesh draws me toward the greed that tightens my fist, the pride that exalts me over the person I seek to help, and the sloth that seeks an easy, less expensive way to give. All acts of charity are susceptible to these vices that cater to my own needs.

All charity should be examined first in motive. Am I loving God and others in my giving, or am I feeding my ego and salving my conscience? "Love covers over a multitude of sins" (1 Peter 4:8; Proverbs 10:12).

My neediness may obscure the true nature of my giving. I may be pouring out affection and feeding my own need at the same time. The need to be useful and significant, my self-affirmation, may blind me to the impact of my acts.

So I must always perform acts of charity with eyes wide open, watching to see that I do no harm as I help another in the presence of my own gaping need. My own needs may be met in the giving while the one I seek to help is left even more in need.

"Love does no harm to its neighbor" (Romans 13:10) is as much a goal as a description of love. It appears in the Latin phrase *primum non nocere*, "first, do no harm," a standard precept for medical ethics. It should also be a standard for charitable giving. Given the circumstances of the wounded, and given our own limitations of understanding, make certain your act of kindness is not harming the one you seek to help.

An emergency medical need may be difficult to diagnose and treat. The same is true of other human needs. But this does not dampen our enthusiasm for the good work. On the contrary, we enter the arena of charity knowing the Band-Aid we place on the wound often has far less healing power than the love that placed it there.

## THE EFFECT OF CARE

Your life can be more interesting, challenging, and rewarding. You can move into a new era of energy and passion. Things can change for you. You are only a few steps away from an adjustment of attitude and outlook that could be powerful and permanent in your life.

You may have received faulty information about the nature and purpose of life on this planet. You may have received what the Apostle Paul described as an "empty way of life handed down to you from your ancestors" (1 Peter 1:18). This feeling of emptiness and futility is the result of a misunderstanding about how life works.

Once implemented, this new approach to living will change the inner condition of your heart and mind.

The same may be said for any social group of which you are a part, including—and especially—your church. No church family will experience the full extent of divine blessings intended and expected without the careful cultivation and disciplined practice of this essential ingredient of believing.

You must care.

Care is both a noun and a verb. With appropriate endings, it converts easily into adverbs and adjectives. The word is versatile and flexible like a rubber band or a twisting tie.

"I don't give a care" seems to express something good.

"Why do you care?" questions the motives and intentions of compassionate words or actions.

And "Who cares?" dismisses people and events with a flick of the hand and a toss of the head.

You will be more like God, and you will experience more divine life and light, if you care. That is The Care Effect.

The effect of caring for another person has four dimensions.

FIRST EFFECT: The Father in Heaven will receive glory from our work. He is pleased when one person cares for another because His character is revealed in that act of love. The Great Commandment has two inseparable parts: love God and love your neighbor. These two are a summation of all the commands that God gives (Matthew 22:35–40).

SECOND EFFECT: I am changed when I care for another person. This is a very predictable and consistent effect of care. This is especially true given the fact that many of us learn by doing rather than by reading a book. In order to actually comprehend and apprehend the gospel, you may need to engage another person in an act of compassion.

THIRD EFFECT: The one who receives care is changed. That change might be dramatic or it may be subtle and hard to see except in retrospect. Every human being can testify to the powerful effect that someone's care for them has had upon their own views and behavior.

FOURTH EFFECT: My world is changed. Caring for others has an effect upon your family, your friendships, your community, and your world. Caring for another human being actually changes the dynamics within a group—relationships, behaviors, speech patterns, and communication. This may be observed in any tightly knit team where one person gives care to another and that caring act becomes public knowledge. You yourself may have been part of a family or classroom or missions group or athletic team in which this occurred. The impact of care travels along relational, friendship, and family lines.

## CARE EFFECT #1: GOD IS PLEASED AND GLORIFIED

*Are not two sparrows sold for a penny? Yet not one of them will fall to the ground outside your Father's care.*
—MATTHEW 10:29

A sparrow is a tiny bird. It is small, brown, and relatively inconspicuous. I do not follow sparrows around tending to their needs. I do not notice when one of them dies. The death of a sparrow does not receive comment in the local newspaper. Yet, these same sparrows are cared for by our Heavenly Father. He knows when one is lost. Jesus of Nazareth says that not one of the sparrows is forgotten before God (Luke 12:6).

Bottom line: God cares. He cares for birds and other animals, and He cares for humans.

Jesus is the one who more than any other teaches us to call God "Father." He teaches us to pray "our Father in heaven." He reminds us continually that God is the Father who watches over us with tender care. This is how He makes God known to us. This is how He impresses us with God's love for us.

83

God is the prototype for fatherhood. He is the First Father. God is also the archetype for fatherhood. He is the True Patriarch. The image of God as father should precede all other images in our minds and imaginations. And it should rule and define "fatherhood" as a concept.

That is not how we experience fatherhood as humans, however. In chronological order and in order of impression, we first experience the presence or absence of our biological fathers. We experience father figures in our lives as infants and preschoolers long before we are able to entertain the abstract notion of an invisible God. These images are very powerful, more powerful in our earliest years than the image or concept of the Creator God as Father.

Jesus is enlivening and rehabilitating the term *father* by calling God our Father in heaven. He is addressing a longing and a hope. He offers to us the God who is the perfect Father, a father whose character and purpose goes beyond any earthly possibility. He is heavenly, this Father, and He is the one who cares for us.

Yet no mention of father falls on our ears without earthly images popping into our minds. To call God "Father" is to make an immediate association for good or ill. Hearing that God is Father conjures up existing images and impressions that cannot be corrected or expunged without some time and work. My sense of God's character is shaped initially by my own experience and understanding of "father."

My earliest memory is a black-and-white mental picture of a large paper bag sitting on the floor between two seats that faced each other. I am standing beside the bag. I know that I was in a passenger car, traveling on a train with my parents. I can feel the motion and sense the changing scenes through the windows above me. I see my parents' forms but not their faces. My brother, Tim, 18 months older than I, is not in this picture. (Sorry, Tim. Maybe you were under the seat, behind the bag, or sitting invisibly on the other side of dad.)

I do not know why this image burned its way permanently into my mental circuitry. Maybe I felt exhilaration, experiencing the strange motion and sound of the train. I do not feel isolation. I am in the presence of my father and mother. I do not feel fear as I stand there by the bag.

My second-oldest memory is another snapshot. I am very young, two or three years old, and my father is carrying me to bed, his left arm under my neck and his right arm under my knees. I woke up for an instant during that brief trip from where I fell asleep in the living room to the bedroom. We passed the hot water heater in the hallway, I remember, and I think it was a narrow hall. I felt completely comfortable and secure, and I fell asleep again before I reached the bed.

This early memory of me in my father's arms looms large. Somehow I pinned that memory permanently on the banner of my mind. I have treasured it all these years, and it has shaped my views of God and the world.

Some people struggle to understand the positive image that Jesus meant to convey when He taught us that God is our Father in heaven. When I worked weekly with women inmates in Texas prisons, I felt compelled to explain the goodness and love of God embedded in that father image. I did not use the term "father" in reference to God without explaining this goodness and love. Most of the female inmates either had no earthly father present in their lives or were abused by their fathers.

Everything in my mind and heart resonated with the image of God as Father from the very first time I heard it. How could it not? From my earliest memory, I was secure and comfortable in my father's arms. It was the perfect picture of God for me, and it remains so to this day. Despite my awareness of the imperfection of my own father and the absence and abuse of many fathers, my own psyche is imprinted by an earthly father who demonstrated profound care for me throughout my life.

Jesus painted a picture of Father Abraham in His story of the rich man and Lazarus, the beggar (Luke 16:19–31). In this story, Lazarus dies and goes to Abraham's side, his bosom. The Greek word designates the front of the body between the arms, the very place where I remember myself being carried by my father. In the afterlife, the poor beggar is in Father Abraham's embrace.

The rich man, lifting up his eyes in hell, asks that Lazarus, who rests in the bosom of Father Abraham, be sent to his father's house to warn his five brothers about the place of torment.

And so Jesus pictures two different fathers and their houses. Father Abraham is in his eternal house with Lazarus, and the rich man's five brothers are in their father's house clueless to their impending doom. The house where the rich man grew up was not a place where he learned of the fatherhood of God.

Jesus does not excuse the rich man or his brothers for their ignorance about eternal things. "They have Moses and the Prophets," He replied to the rich man's request. "Let them listen to them" (v. 29).

The issue here is repentance: "If someone from the dead goes to them," the rich man says, his five brothers "will repent" (v. 30). Repentance involves a change of mind. These brothers, like the rich man himself, are self-absorbed. They are thinking only of today, its comforts and benefits. They have not contemplated or acknowledged the eternal consequences of their choices. Repentance would involve the abandonment of their way of life and the choice of a new course and direction based upon the care of God for them and their care of others.

The Heavenly Father's care for us includes an amazing invitation—to live in the Father's house and to be seated at his table. Jesus paints such a picture of our future as God's children. He told His disciples, "My Father's house has many rooms . . . I am going there to prepare a place for you" (John 14:2). He said "the kingdom of heaven is like a king who prepared a wedding banquet for his son" (Matthew 22:2). He sends out his servants to gather all the guests: "Go to the street corners and invite to the banquet anyone you find" (v. 9).

## REFLECTIONS

1. Do you have an early memory of your father?
2. How does the picture of God as the Heavenly Father work for you?
3. How would you explain the term "Father" for those who grew up without a father or were abused by their fathers?

## THE FATHER'S HOUSE

My childhood home sat on a street called Easy Way, the end of which seemed always in danger of being washed away. The dry riverbed of the *arroyo* made a turn to the right and snaked around the barrier at the end of the road, then turned west and continued its path to the Rio Grande River only half a mile away. The paved road turned to dirt right in front of our house. It took a hard right, got a new name, and ran along the *arroyo* gouged into the earth by rushing water from the mountain rains.

Sand and grease wood stretched east from my bedroom window for miles, finally running up the western slopes of the Franklin Mountains and turning into a thousand shades of purple as sand gave way to tumbled stone on the flanks of those towering peaks. When I wasn't hiking in those mountains and exploring old mineshafts, I was dreaming about doing it.

I stepped into the desert whenever I left the house on Easy Way. In fact, our home was an extension of the desert, built from the purple stones carried down from the mountains by way of the *arroyo*. The mortar, too, was desert produce. I shook the screen as a five-year-old, sifting the sand we collected from the *arroyo*, capturing the grease wood leaves and pebbles. Dad made the mortar from that sifted sand.

Dad created the concrete slab of our house slowly with a hundred loads from a battered cement mixer. A single pour didn't seem to make a dent in the large area of sand defined by concrete peers and enclosed by wooden forms. It seemed to me that mixer growled and churned continually. The little finger of my left hand still sports a scar from a careless moment near its metal gears.

Dad would stab his spade into a bag of gray powder, toss the cement into the orange mouth of the mixer as it turned, and match it with three spades of gravel, straight from the *arroyo*. Gravel, sand, and stones from the desert were captured, modified, and organized to create our home on Easy Way. For my father, there was nothing easy about it.

I never mowed the grass on Easy Way. I don't think we owned a mower. The yard was sand and rocks. Periodically, instead of mowing we raked rocks into rows and piles, then loaded the wheelbarrow and poured them into the *arroyo*. We had a chicken coop in the backyard and a clothesline—two metal poles with a crossbar and three strands of wire. I can see my mother now, surrounded by colorful clothes, bending over a plastic basket full of wet laundry, flickering in and out of my vision as the breeze blew sheets and towels.

Our family lived in this house on Easy Way for six of my most formative years in two different stints. Among the houses we made into home through my boyhood, this is the one I remember most fondly and consider above others to be my father's house.

## THE FATHER'S TABLE SERVICE

*Jesus saith unto them, "Come and dine."*
—JOHN 21:12 (KJV)

My father's voice carried in the desert air. I could hear him singing even if I had wandered some distance from the house. When I heard the first notes of "Come and Dine," I forsook the pursuit of lizards and horned toads and ran home. "Come and Dine" was the announcement that dinner was ready. I started singing as I ran. We all knew the song, and the sound would swell as the family gathered until it resounded clearly in four-part harmony for even neighbors to hear. We all felt compelled to sing. It was our announcement that we, too, were part of this family.

The rectangular dining table was a slab of wood with a leg at each corner. Our younger brother, Joe, was a nuisance to us older boys. We caught him, carried him, and stretched him, spread-eagled, under the table one morning, securing his limbs with belts and ropes to each of the wooden legs. The table was too heavy for him to move, and we were delighted that it took some time for mother to come to his rescue. He thrashed and screamed, staring up at the bottom of that table, and we laughed and laughed, hidden around the corner.

The discipline was meted out fairly and firmly. Our dinner table was not to be used to subdue one another. We did not wrestle at the table. We did not vanquish our foes there. We served one another at the table.

My father made two long benches out of 2-by-12 pine planks. They were sturdy, and they provided most of the seating at our dining table for many years. I know for sure that we could seat six children on one bench, maybe seven.

Our parents made sure that mealtime was special. We sang our way to the table, and then we always offered thanks. Guests were never refused a seat at the table, even when times were hard. Homemade bread—loaves and rolls—and mashed potatoes served in a roasting pan were staples along with fried chicken and pinto beans.

My father was the host at mealtime, and mother was the hostess. Reflecting back on my boyhood, I realize that my mother spent an inordinate amount of time in the kitchen preparing meals for her large family. On Mondays, we would find her there kneading dough, separating it into loaves and rolls, placing the pans of rising dough all over the kitchen, and baking the bread. I saw her pushing strands of brown hair away from her face with her forearm as she worked. Her hands were covered with flour. I never thought about the taxing nature of her task until I was an adult trying to knead some dough.

Dad would usually announce that the meal was ready. He would begin the singing that called the family to the table. He would lead in prayer or call on one of us to do so. We all learned early to pray the prayer of blessing at mealtime. Dad would announce things to the family gathered at the table. He was in charge of decorum at the table, such as it was. We grew up knowing it was his table.

The experience at the table always seemed rich in love, gratitude, joy, and fellowship even though the meals were mostly beans, bread, and potatoes. The security provided by loving parents was enough to transform even simple fare into a feast.

The single piece of furniture required for a Christian church is a table. The Lord's Supper—communion—is best observed with a table. All my life I have helped carry, tug, and position the communion table in and around the sanctuary. Sometimes the table is a wooden box, awkward to move, with the words, "Do this in remembrance of me," carved on its face. Sometimes it is a simple wooden surface with four exposed legs and no decorative features. But some kind of table is required for the bread and the cup in the meal of remembrance.

The table is the single piece of furniture in any home that positions the family face to face. It turns our ears and eyes toward one another. It fosters and even forces conversation. At the table we either reinforce our love for one another or encounter the barriers and wounds that keep us apart.

Those long benches of my boyhood forced us to sit elbow to elbow. We were required to pass the potatoes, the butter, and the bread. We were serving one another even though we did not think about it much. But in the serving of one another we built the bond of fellowship and love. We cared for each other at the table and that very fact changed us.

## REFLECTIONS

1. Describe mealtime at your home of origin.
2. When are you most uncomfortable at a table?
3. Do you think God will really have a big table in heaven? What does the talk about a heavenly banquet mean to you?

## JESUS AT MEALTIME

The scriptural story behind the gospel song "Come and Dine" is the post-resurrection appearance of Jesus on the shore of the Sea of Galilee (John 21). The apostles are there because Peter said, "I'm going fishing." I suppose it was all he knew to do in the wake of his denial of the Lord Jesus. Peter suffered from the deepest shame and self-condemnation. He had deserted and denied Jesus at His trial and Crucifixion. Peter was lost in the wake of his failure, unable to recover, and so he returned to the life he knew before he met Jesus. Failure in following Jesus may make any of us try to do this.

The apostles fished all night and caught nothing. Early in the morning Jesus appeared on the shore and suggested they cast their nets on the right side of the boat. When they did, they caught such a huge number of fish they were unable even to get the nets back into the boat. That is when they knew it was the Lord Jesus.

The risen Lord Jesus in His glorified body had scrambled around the shoreline, found some wood, and started a fire. He had bread, and fish were cooking in the flames. He invited them, "Come and dine," and they sat down for breakfast, presumably in a circle around the fire.

This meal was planned and served by Jesus. Evidently, it was a moment of great importance for Him. He did for Peter here at breakfast what Peter could not do for himself. Jesus prompted Peter to a three-fold confession of love, one confession for each of the three denials. Then Jesus instructed him to "feed my sheep." He reinstated Peter as the leader of the group. This is how Jesus used this breakfast. He found His own lost sheep and brought him back into the fold.

"Feed my sheep," Jesus said (v. 17). This instruction from Jesus to the leader of the apostles could be more literal than we have generally thought. Twice Jesus instructed Peter to "feed" His sheep, and once, in the middle and in parallel, Jesus used the term that is translated "take care of." Our usual definitions of these two terms in this context are spiritual in nature—teaching and tending the flock. But what if Jesus also had in mind the literal meal of fellowship and the meal of remembrance that would immediately become part of Christian gatherings? At the beginning of the Last Supper, Jesus said to them, "I have eagerly desired to eat this Passover with you before I suffer" (Luke 22:15). It loomed large in His mind, this final Passover with His disciples, and He anticipated it with a hope and longing born out of His love for them.

Mealtimes were important to Jesus. They provided the key setting for significant interaction, instruction, and bonding with his friends. At the Last Supper, Jesus created what we now call the Lord's Supper, a ceremony that He clearly instructed us to keep observing as a way of remembering Him.

The gatherings in the wake of the coming of the Holy Spirit were distinguished by "the breaking of bread" (Acts 2:42). The disciples met every day, house to house, and "ate together with glad and sincere hearts" (Acts 2:46). These references to mealtime involved both the fellowship meal, their version of a "covered dish," and the observance of the meal of remembrance with the passing of the bread and the cup.

The Gospel writers tell us that Jesus was a preacher. But they never picture Him behind a pulpit or a speaker's stand. Jesus is pictured sitting down in a boat or on a hillside, but He is never described as sitting in a chair (until He sits down at the right hand of the Father in heaven). Jesus is described lying in a manger as a baby and lying on the ground in prayer. But He is never pictured lying in a bed.

However, several times in the Gospels Jesus is present at a table. He reclined at the table in the home of Simon the Pharisee. He was at the table in Mary and Martha's house. He reclined at the table with His disciples in the Upper Room. This is where He instituted the meal, the Supper, that became and remains a fixture of Christian worship.

Jesus also ended up at a table with the two disciples whom He joined on the Road to Emmaus after His resurrection (Luke 24: 13–35). They did not know who He was until He broke the bread at the table. When people are walking along the road they do not usually face one another. They are all looking forward as they travel. But when they gather at the table, they face one another and see each other. Jesus broke the bread, and the disciples saw for the first time the wounds of the nails in His hands. They discovered His true identity at the table.

We often reveal more of ourselves and see more of others at the table than any other time. This is why Jesus insisted that a meal with bread and wine be part of our regular gatherings, so that we might see Him and one another more clearly.

## MEALTIME FOR THE SAINTS

Jesus told us plainly that there is a table in heaven where the saints of God will gather. Our family gathering song, "Come and Dine," was written by Charles B. Widmeyer in 1906. It begins with these words: "Jesus has a table spread where the saints of God are fed. He invites his chosen people, 'Come and dine.'" Growing up I always felt these words were a reference to the heavenly feast that we will enjoy one day when this earthly life is over and our life in heaven begins.

The communion table is a symbol of God's care for us. We remember at the table all that God has done in Christ to rescue us from our sins. We remember the suffering of the Savior on our behalf and how He served the disciples in the upper room. We allow the Savior to serve us when we come to the Lord's table during worship.

The communion table is also a symbol of how we serve one another. The bread and cup are delivered to the worshipers. They receive the elements and serve those who sit beside them. We may be sitting in rows of chairs or pews, but we pass the elements of the meal just as my brothers and I passed the food to one another sitting on our benches at the table. As we pass around the bread and cup in worship, we are expressing the care and love for one another that Jesus insists will distinguish us upon this earth.

Jesus told a story about a rich man, well-clothed and well-fed, and a beggar named Lazarus who lay at his gate covered with sores (Luke 16:21). The poor beggar longed to feed himself with the scraps that fell from the rich man's table. The spiritual destitution of the rich man and his eventual condemnation to hell is apparent only in this fact—he did not serve the beggar at his table.

Sitting down at the table to eat together is an intimate event. Who knows where this food came from? Who knows how it was prepared? Who knows if these hands and utensils are sanitary? Have you ever sat down at the table with a beggar covered with sores? Would you enjoy such an experience? Would you eat the food on your plate?

Many cultures protect mealtime. Most religions have specific guidelines about what to eat and how to eat and with whom to eat. Jesus scandalized the religious leaders of His day by enjoying table fellowship with tax collectors and "sinners." This practice rendered him unclean, according to their calculations, and showed care and love for people who really did not seem to them to deserve it.

Jesus pushed Peter and the other disciples into Gentile homes and even to their tables for meals. They did not want to go there. God sent Peter a vision of new mealtime rules at the house in Joppa (Acts 10:9–34). God instructed him to eat things that he had judged all his life to be unclean. Then a knock came at the door. Gentiles stood there, and they invited Peter to the home of Cornelius. The gospel of Christ jumped across the greatest divide between people in the ancient world. Peter spent time in the home of a Roman soldier, and everyone there trusted in Jesus as Savior.

Table fellowship with Gentiles would continue to be an issue for many years in the early church. Even Peter slid back from the lesson he learned at the house of Cornelius and refused to eat with Gentiles (Galatians 2:12). The Lord Jesus had torn down the barrier between Jew and Gentile. He had made the two one in his death upon the Cross. The practical outworking of this truth, however, was difficult for all involved.

Most of us have a feeling that some group of people is "unclean." It may have to do with their ethnicity or their economic standing or their physical appearance. We may have such strong feelings about certain people that we find them revolting. The idea of eating with them at the same table makes us lose our appetite.

This feeling of revulsion toward other human beings made in the image of God does not reflect the heart of Jesus. Acknowledging this truth is one step toward healing the breach between us. Serving one another is an even more important step. Jesus insists that His church enjoy table fellowship, putting aside all cultural and ethnic barriers, because this expresses His love lavished upon all people. When we serve one another at the table, we are following the example of Jesus. Although it may violate longstanding attitudes and cultural norms, we must do it because Jesus is Lord and this is His table.

## REFLECTIONS

1. Why is mealtime so important to Jesus?
2. Why did Jesus establish a meal as part of worship?
3. Do you know any groups that you consider "unclean" and would have a hard time breaking bread with?

## GOD AS WAITER

None of us can fully comprehend the love of God. It surpasses our understanding. Jesus' description of God's fatherhood is His consistent effort to communicate the depth and breadth of God's love. The culmination of this expression will come in heaven when, according to the parable of Jesus, the faithful servants will be seated at the Father's table and He Himself will dress for service and wait on them (Luke 12:37).

I confess a great reluctance to accept the idea that God Himself would put on the servant's uniform and serve me. Like Peter, I protest: "You shall never wash my feet!" (John 13:8). God has configured this universe in such a way that love is made evident in service. The care and service I extend to those around me is the clearest indication that I have received by faith the Father's love and care for me.

Would the God of this universe don a waiter's garb, lay a towel across His forearm, and serve me at His table? That proposition is so far outside our own norms and values that it seems ridiculous. Were it a stand-alone illustration of the character of God we might dismiss it with some creative exegesis of the text.

This picture of the Creator God serving us is not isolated, however. It is pervasive in the teachings of Jesus and throughout the Bible. God serves us in our sickness like a nurse bustling around our bed. God serves us in our sorrow, bringing us comfort and consolation. God serves us in our salvation, delivering us from sin with the death of His one and only Son upon the Cross. God continues to serve us in our sanctification, washing our feet every day, showing us the path to real life and peace.

Many people never get this message about the nature of God and the nature of true life. We are so captured by a conception of the universe revolving around us that we cannot break free even to contemplate such an other-centered world.

My friend, Beth Akin, ends her emails with this quote: "I slept and dreamt that life was joy. I awoke and saw that life was service. I acted and behold, service was joy" (Rabindranath Tagore). True life flows out of service, and service is joy. This is how the universe is ordered because this is the character of God.

He is glorified and pleased when we learn to follow Him in serving others.

## THE FATHER'S ROOM SERVICE

*"In my father's house are many rooms."*
—JOHN 14:2 KJV

My dad built a house with many rooms—six bedrooms, to be exact. He added a back porch later that could also be used as a bedroom.

I got married the summer he built that house in 1972. Before I married, however, and after I finished the semester at Baylor University, Dad recruited me to help with the house raising. And I was happy to do so, as were four of my brothers.

We bought a load of supplies that included 12-foot-long 2-by-6 boards, many sheets of plywood, and some concrete blocks. We pulled the trailer into the tall grass of a 40-acre pasture Dad had purchased. I assumed that Dad knew exactly where he wanted the house positioned, but I did not see any stakes that marked the spot.

We started immediately to nail together those boards, creating six 12-foot square grids with floor joists on 16-inch centers. We raised the first grid above the ground, mounting it on concrete blocks. We leveled that grid in both directions, the tall grass waving in the breeze through and above the boards.

We nailed the grids together, leveling with the concrete blocks and wooden shims as we moved from left to right. The house was to be 36 feet wide and 24 feet deep. Dad may have had a drawing somewhere, but I did not see it.

When the six grids were securely fastened one to another and leveled and squared from corner to corner, we decked that entire grid of boards with half-inch plywood, creating the floor of the house. We began immediately to raise the walls in much the same fashion.

This was my father's approach to many things. He expended little time on details. He did only meager planning and preparation. He lunged into things and created order out of the chaos. He was like those artists who do chalk talks. They sketch things on the board, and you wonder what in the world they are making. The design they had in mind all along eventually emerges.

My brother-in-law famously characterized a Crosby vacation: "You load the kids in the car, strap the luggage on top, pull down the driveway, and stop at the curb. Then Dad says, 'Which way do you want to turn?'"

It was exhilarating, growing up that way. We lived in the moment. Life was spontaneous.

The house, however, was never quite finished. It served the family well for many years, but Dad never got to the trim work. The family moved into a house with plywood floors and no doorknobs. That was fine. We never expected things to be fancy. Among the homes that we lived in during my boyhood, this one ranked high. It was bigger than most, and it had two bathrooms. Hurray!

The Father in heaven gives us life that is exhilarating, but He is also good with details. His house of many rooms is perfectly designed for each of us. The word translated "mansions" in the King James Version is used only twice in the Greek New Testament, in John 14:2 and John 14:23. In the first instance the word refers to the abode or dwelling that the Father in heaven has provided for us—"In my Father's house are many mansions." In the second instance, Jesus said that He and the Father would come to us and make their abode (mansion) with us.

Home is important to most fathers. And it is important to the Father in heaven. Most fathers want their children gathered around them. Jesus taught us that the Father in heaven is planning this for our eternity with Him.

We mimic the Heavenly Father when we care for others. We bring Him glory, and He is pleased. No wonder the Great Command is love God and love neighbor.

## CARE EFFECT #2: I AM CHANGED

God is in the business of shaping me, making me more like Himself, for we "are being transformed into his image" (2 Corinthians 3:18). When I am a disciple in motion, putting one foot in front of the other as I travel to places I have never been before, God has the opportunity to change my thinking, my whole perspective—even my understanding of the gospel.

This happens to me as part of the Care Effect. I am changed both by giving care and by receiving care. I can trace this truth in my life all the way back to some of my earliest memories.

I have this picture of me and my family when I was five years old. I am standing on a sidewalk in a row with four of my brothers. Our rock house on Easy Way is in the background. I am dressed in a sailor suite with the white scarf and jacket. My four brothers and my parents are dressed in ordinary clothes.

*The Crosby family circa 1958*

I don't look happy about my outfit, really. I was old enough to be particular about clothing. But the look is distinctive, and it has a message embedded in it that made a difference to me as a boy and left a lasting impression. That message was this: you have value and potential.

I got this message from a young woman named Mary who decided to give me special attention. I was the second of five boys who came to my parents in rapid succession. Mary "adopted" me, I suppose, and gave me the gift of care as a little boy. She was a teenager when she first met our family. She attended my father's first church in Oylen, Minnesota. She was our babysitter.

Mary lived with us during a brief stint in Maryland when my father took a pastoral position there. When we then moved to serve a mission church in El Paso, Mary came to visit.

Mac was a soldier stationed at Fort Bliss. He attended our church, and he and Dad became great friends. He helped my father build our home on the outskirts of El Paso. Dad bought an old Army truck, and he and Mac, with a little help from me and my brothers, turned the stones and gravel they found in the *arroyos* into concrete, mortar, and rock walls. You can see their stone work in the photograph of our family at the time. I remember that rock house as the best among our childhood homes.

My match-making mother invited Mary for an extended stay in El Paso. She remembers pushing Mary up the stairs at a fellowship meeting, insisting that she meet Mac. They fell in love, had a whirlwind romance, and were married for 51 years and had four children.

"Mary asked about you," my mother said with a smile many years later. "You were always her favorite." I smiled, too. Mac and Mary never fully exited the orbit of our family. My parents stayed in touch with them and visited them in their home in Colorado. They were lifelong friends, but I had not seen them since I was a boy.

I saw Mary and Mac for the first time in nearly 50 years at the 60th wedding anniversary of my parents. I saw them again in the crowd as the family exited First Baptist Church of Gatesville after the memorial service for Dad. The hall was crowded. They were two faces in a sea of faces. Something stopped me in my tracks when I spied them as our family was processing toward the hearse. I stepped up to them, put both my arms around their necks, and hugged them close. I said, "Thank you for loving us when we were little. It made a big difference." The urge just came over me, and I surprised them with a hug.

A few hours later, Mary and Mac, making their way home from my father's funeral, were involved in a collision with an 18-wheeler that ended both their lives. Mary died at the scene, and Mac died a week later never having regained consciousness.

My spontaneous act of affection for them was rooted in their care for me when I was a preschooler. I spoke my heart to them, prompted by a spirit of gratitude.

And it was the last word I shared with them on this earth.

Mary left her fingerprints on my heart. I think they are still pretty deep. She cared for me when I was one of five little boys, and I have not forgotten that care. She built a bridge from her heart to mine. And she still remembered me more than 50 years later, and wanted to know how I was doing. Mother said, "Mary always asks about you."

Researchers now tell us that this kind of love actually changes the way the brain develops in a child. The brain of a child who experiences abandonment and abuse develops differently than those who receive consistent love and affection. Brain scans performed on abandoned children have revealed how trauma hinders brain development. Relational strategies have been identified for intervention with traumatized children (see the work of Dr. Karyn Purvis and Dr. David Cross at Texas Christian University's Institute of Child Development). These strategies involve consistent and unconditional connection, love, and care.

Literally, receiving care from another person changes me, especially when I am young.

Think of all the ways we can touch the little ones. Our foster care ministry at FBNO will bear fruit for generations on this earth as well as forever in heaven. Our Sunday Schools, camps, Vacation Bible Schools, tutoring, and children's sports ministries are some of our most important work.

We send sunbeams far down the path when we love little ones. We can verify this simply by thinking about our own childhood and how our lives were shaped by the absence or presence of caring individuals who lavished us with love.

## REFLECTIONS

1. Did any adults apart from relatives leave a lasting and positive impression on you as a child? How? Have you thanked them?
2. Do you have a personal ministry with any children? If so, please describe it.
3. How could you and your church increase the impact you have upon children at risk in your community?

## LEARNING TO LOVE ON SKID ROW

My family frequently traveled a road that ran along the Rio Grande River between El Paso and Juarez, Mexico. Fifty years later I can still see the tall, shiny buildings of downtown El Paso glistening in the sun—and the cardboard shacks on the hillside across the river. I remember the contrast between the two cities and wondered as a boy why a border would make so much difference.

I saw children and adults swimming and washing clothes in the muddy, shallow river. I knew that these people could not wash their clothes at home, that the cardboard-and-plastic shelters that dotted the downslope to the river had no utilities at all. We were living through one of our family's hardest economic times, with my father working odd jobs to make ends meet. But I knew we were rich compared to our neighbors across the border.

Visiting an orphanage in Juarez I learned something of the desperation of poverty. We sang for a little girl who was deliberately blinded by her mother shortly after birth so that she could beg more effectively. Her mother rubbed hot peppers in her eyes, they told us. Even today I remember the children who gathered around us—children who had food and clothes and shelter only because Christian people cared enough to provide for them.

My first missions trip, so to speak, was a week-long foray into the area south of Juarez. We traveled from village to village, sleeping in a car or in buildings made available by the churches. We worked with pastors who cared for small congregations. We watched as career missionaries ministered to the crowds who came. I was 12 years old, and my perception of the world was changing.

When I was even younger, a missionary came to our church and taught us a song about the Good Samaritan. I don't know who wrote it, and I cannot find it anywhere on the Internet. But here are the words I learned:

> *On the other side of the road,*
> *The sick and wounded lie.*
> *They're calling for help and for mercy.*
> *Oh, how can you pass them by?*
>
> *The Savior asks your love*
> *In the service of want and pain.*
> *And anything more that thou spendest*
> *He'll pay when He comes again.*

The kindly missionary who taught us that song spent time with us. He seemed old and gentle to me. He lived in a strange place far away where he taught people about God's love. During a worship service he touched my shoulder and invited me to pray with him, which I did. I don't remember what I prayed as we knelt side-by-side at the front of the church. But I do remember how he noticed me, cared for me, and wanted me to learn about the love of God and neighbor as described in Jesus' story of the Good Samaritan and the song that he taught us.

One of my father's self-made ministry appointments was at the rescue mission in downtown El Paso. It was an independent ministry, as I recall, with sleeping quarters on the second floor and a large dining hall next to the chapel on the first floor. We ate dinner in the dining hall after leading the worship service in the chapel, sitting on long benches with the crowd of strangers who were residents for the evening.

A middle-aged woman stood by two small pasteboard boxes in front of the mission as we drove up one day. She was left alone on the sidewalk as a vehicle's trunk was closed and the driver sped away. She wore dark shoes and a light-colored dress that reached almost to her ankles. Her hair was captured in a colorful handkerchief. She surveyed her surroundings, then bent over and picked up one of the boxes.

I think about her now and then—who she was and why she was seeking shelter at the mission that day. I assumed those boxes contained all her belongings. I look past her in my mind's eye and see the street sign anchored in concrete at the corner. Dad said that the mission was on "Skid Row." That's not what the sign said. I looked all around one day for a sign that said "Skid Row" and couldn't find it. I slowly came to the realization that the street itself bore another name, but all the clients lived figuratively on Skid Row.

My brothers and I, coached by our father, sang gospel songs *a cappella* in four-part harmony. Even though I protested, Dad insisted that I sing. He taught me to sing bass an octave higher. At 12 years of age, I could hit the high notes, not the low ones. We worked at home every day to learn the songs and our individual parts. It became a delightful part of our lives as brothers. We sang together in the car, on the street, when we played, and when we went to church.

We sang *a cappella* even though my mother knew how to play the piano, and a large upright piano sat right there on the platform at the mission. Dad wanted us to emphasize the harmonies, to pick out the notes and create the music with only our voices. Mother was often at the mission, but she was always occupied with our younger brothers and sisters. She assisted Dad in teaching us to sing and gave us notes one by one on the piano. She often played when Dad led music at the mission or at churches. But we sang without accompaniment because Dad preferred it that way. Many years later, that is how our family sang for hours around him as he died.

At the mission, we four brothers stood in a row on the platform beside the wooden pulpit and sang the songs Dad taught us. The chapel seemed like a wooden box to me—wooden platform, wooden pews, and wooden doors. Reflecting on it now I realize it was a great place to sing without amplification. The crowd seemed surprised and delighted. We sang without restraint, fueled by the crowd's response, loving the sound we created together, making music together as boys.

Dad opened his Bible and brought a gospel message. He was a great preacher, my father, full of passion for Christ. He created vivid images that brought Bible passages to life. He often pulled away from his big family, found a secluded spot in the house or the outdoors, and lost himself in meditation with his Bible open in his hands or on his lap. His messages took shape as he worked the Scripture through his mind and heart. And his gift of language gave wings to those thoughts.

He always closed his message with an invitation for people to respond to Christ. We brothers joined those who came to the kneeling bench at the front, and we prayed with them. Sometimes those who responded smelled of alcohol, a strange smell to me. Their faces were flushed, their eyes yellow. I learned these were indications of chronic alcohol consumption. I prayed with them even if they were drunk. Who needs God more than a drunken stranger staying at the mission?

This is part of my story, my boyhood. I sang to the homeless and orphans as planned by my father on earth and my Father in heaven. My perception of the world was shaped by these experiences.

Most of us have similar stories to tell of receiving and giving care. In the midst of these interchanges we became the people we are today.

## REFLECTIONS

1. Did you ever come in contact with homeless people when you were a child? If so, how?
2. Have you visited or worked in rescue missions or homeless shelters? Are these kinds of facilities part of your volunteer activity, giving, or prayer life?

3. How do you think you might connect with the homeless population in your area?

## COMPLICATED HOSPITALITY

The hospitality of the Father and the Son, the preparation of a place for us in heaven, is loaded with meaning for our own journey on this planet.

Loving our neighbor involves hospitality. The Good Samaritan was hospitable to the wounded man. He took him to an inn. He stayed with him overnight. He provided extended lodging for him. He assured the innkeeper that he would take care of any extra expenses when he returned. He addressed both present and future needs for the wounded man.

Extending hospitality to strangers is part of loving our neighbors and following Christ. Jesus Himself benefited from the hospitality of friends. While He had no place to call His own, He often stayed in the home of Mary, Martha, and Lazarus.

Our responsibility to care for strangers is clear from the beginning to the end of the Bible. The children of Israel were to care for strangers: "Do not mistreat or oppress a foreigner, for you were foreigners in Egypt" (Exodus 22:21). When the law was given to Moses, it included this instruction about strangers.

The Great Commandment actually originated in the instructions concerning foreigners. "The foreigner residing among you must be treated as your native-born. Love them as yourself, for you were foreigners in Egypt. I am the LORD your God" (Leviticus 19:34). Jesus taught us to "Love your neighbor as yourself" (Matthew 22:39).

The early church understood the obligation to care for one another. "Do not forget to show hospitality to strangers, for by so doing some people have shown hospitality to angels without knowing it" (Hebrews 13:2). Hospitality is certainly a gift that some people possess. They love to care for others by receiving them into their homes.

Hospitality is also an obligation for all God's people whether we have this special endowment or not. Caring for neighbors involves helping with the basic necessities of life—clothing, food, and shelter.

The hospitality that the church of Jesus Christ extended to refugees of Hurricane Katrina was startling to behold. It is still a subject of conversation today among those of us who evacuated in the face of the great storm. When we talk about Katrina, we talk about the many people who opened their homes and hearts to us.

Eighty percent of the homes in our neighborhood flooded as a result of Hurricane Katrina. Our home did not flood nor did our immediate neighbors. A total of seven families lived for months in our home, the home to our north, and the home across the street from us. Multiple families lived in many of the homes that did not flood. Both of our daughters' families lost their homes to Hurricane Katrina, and both of their families spent time in our house.

My wife and I were shown hospitality in places like Minden, Louisiana, and Mullin, Texas. We stayed with strangers for weeks. When we got back home, we were able to extend hospitality to others. More than 100 people stayed in our home over the course of the first year after the great flood in New Orleans.

Showing hospitality can be complicated.

A group of men from a Texas church came to New Orleans to help clean out flooded homes. The crew included one man who was homeless but who wanted to come to our city and help us recover. After pleading with the pastor, he was allowed to join the team. He wanted to stay in New Orleans when the team went back home, but I insisted that he return with his team. In its devastated condition immediately after the flood, our city was no place for the homeless.

The crew slept upstairs, mostly in what we called the music room. The former owners' children had surprised their mother while she was away for a week, and invited the television show "While You Were Out" to convert the bonus room over the garage into a small theater. They installed a stage for her drum set, painted stars on the blue ceiling, and surrounded the room with ropes of running lights. We used it as a kind of bunkhouse in the rebuilding years after Katrina. That windowless space seems like a cave, dark and silent—a great place to sleep.

Our daughter, Rebekah, and her husband were staying in one of the upstairs bedrooms at the time. Everyone used the little half bath downstairs when the upstairs bathroom was occupied.

The homeless man came to the breakfast table on that final morning as they made plans to depart. Most of the men had finished eating and were enjoying another cup of coffee. Janet prepared a breakfast of eggs, bacon, and biscuits for the late arrival.

"Good morning," he said as he pulled up a chair, and the six or eight men around the table greeted him. He was the last one to roll out of bed that morning. He looked disheveled to me with his hair uncombed, his stubbly beard, his clothes wrinkled, and his smile accented by missing teeth and lots of pink gum. I guessed him to be 60 years old.

"Say, pastor, thank you for the use of the toothbrush," he said to me, offhand, and he took another bite of breakfast. The comment knit my brows for a moment.

"Toothbrush?" I responded, with only a tinge of alarm, pressing back in my chair. "What toothbrush?"

"Oh, I've been using that toothbrush in the little bathroom down here."

I swallowed hard and caught Janet looking at me, wide-eyed. We both knew immediately whose toothbrush that was. Rebekah had moved to the downstairs half bath with part of her early morning routine when this crew arrived, including moving her toothbrush and toothpaste.

I hunched over my coffee and smothered the laughter that was trying to bubble out of me. My shoulders may have been shaking a little, stifling the mirth, and I could see that Janet was struggling, too, watching me shake and thinking about our snaggle-toothed guest borrowing a toothbrush. Unwittingly, Rebekah had been sharing her toothbrush with a homeless man for a week.

Rebekah wasn't at the table when this conversation occurred, and we didn't say anything to her for a long time. What was the point? When we finally told her this story she grimaced, then grinned.

Showing hospitality to strangers is one certain way to increase the risk, pain, surprise, and reward in the journey of life. In this regard it is similar to all of our efforts to extend love to our neighbors. Loving people is just a risky, messy business. You never know all that will be involved, and you are generally surprised by the twists and turns that come. The reward of love may be increased pain and sorrow. Sometimes love is the conduit for rich humor and laughter that breaks like waves upon the soul. The ultimate effect of our care for others is to broaden and deepen the experience of living in all its dimensions.

As Jesus said of loving God and neighbor, "Do this and you will live" (Luke 10:28).

## REFLECTIONS

1. Do you think the call of Christ on your life involves any personal risk?
2. What do you think about this idea of hospitality—caring for strangers? Would you ever do it?
3. Can you imagine any rewards that would come to you as a result of extending hospitality to strangers?

BLINDERS AND BRIEF ENCOUNTERS

Do you think the Good Samaritan ever "hung out" with the man who fell among thieves? I mean, after that emotional rescue on the road, did the two of them develop an enduring friendship? Did they become part of the same faith community or share dinner on a weekly basis?

I know the question is a little strange. It's like wondering if Snow White and Prince Charming had children or if Samwise Gamgee went on another adventure after being mayor of the Shire. The question goes beyond the original storyteller's limits.

I am speculating about two people who are fictional figures in a parable of Jesus. But it is a special story, after all, this tale that Jesus tells in answer to the question, "Who is my neighbor?" It stands out even in the magnificent collection of parables told by Jesus.

Indulge me for a moment. Did the two key persons in the parable develop a continuing relationship? What do you think?

My guess is that they did not. Their lives intersected on the road between Jerusalem and Jericho at a time when one of them was in great need and the other was able and willing to help. They walked together briefly. They never forgot each other. They parted finally as friends and never saw each other again.

Their lives continued, but on different trajectories.

Such is the nature of life on this planet. Very few people travel with us for the entire expanse of our existence here—siblings, cousins, and select friends, maybe. Some people travel with us for an era of our lives—childhood, adolescence, young adulthood, the empty nest.

Most people we meet and get to know are short-term in our lives. We may not want it that way, either one of us. But in the end, life moves them on or moves us on. We do not usually have a formal, final parting. Our lives simply continue on custom-made tracks that do not intersect again.

These encounters with other persons, brief though they may be, are full of amazing opportunities: the opportunity to live out what we say we believe, the opportunity to help someone in need, the opportunity to leave for a time the track we always travel, and the opportunity to catch a glimpse of a world dramatically different from our own.

Imagine the poverty of our experience on this planet if all we ever knew was what we shared with lifelong traveling companions. That custom-made track would truly be a rut—a deep and narrow and elongated indention in the earth that looks pretty much the same from beginning to end, like a grave with both ends knocked out of it. If we never engage in a significant way with persons whose lives are dramatically different from our own, then we are cursed with blinders.

Blinders are the circular pieces of leather mounted on the heads of horses or mules. Blinders eliminate the animal's peripheral vision. The person driving the buggy does not have blinders, of course. He can see all around. The horse, however, is a draft animal whose life is confined to a simple task on a repetitive track. The blinders prevent the horse from being distracted by events that are not germane to his solitary role in life—pulling that buggy. Often the horse with blinders is depicted plodding along, "clip-clop," dull and bored, head drooping, back swayed. His single initiative in life may be snatching a blade of grass that has forced its way through a crack in the road. Life is colorless and uninteresting, reduced to tunnel vision.

Horses dream, I expect, just like dogs and cats. They wake up startled and disoriented because they have been on mental journeys.

Maybe horses dream about prancing at the front of parades or chasing the wind through canyons, manes flying. Draft horses wearing blinders may dream of seeing things they never see and doing things they never do.

When you wear blinders, you have literally seen it all before.

People wear blinders, though not usually on purpose. The things that give us grounding in life—family heritage, shared culture, common language and education, economic stability—also work like boundaries or borders in our vision and understanding. They can and do become blinders that prevent us from seeing the world from another point of view. Sometimes we live with the impression that we ourselves are the center of the world, that there is nothing of importance or value beyond our blinders. We are content to see today only what we have seen before, and to do it again and again.

Right before telling the story of the Good Samaritan, Jesus told His questioner, the expert in the moral law, "Do this and you will live" (Luke 10:28). The expert wanted to know what to do in order to inherit eternal life. He wanted to live forever, and he supposed that some activity on his part would earn him eternal life.

Jesus threw the question back at him: "What is written in the Law? . . . How do you read it?" (v. 26). That is the moment that

Gospel-writer Luke actually introduces the Great Commandment. The expert in the law came up with the Great Commandment in response to the question of Jesus, "How do you read it?"

The expert replied, "'Love the Lord your God with all your heart and with all your soul and with all your strength and with all your mind'; and, 'Love your neighbor as yourself'" (v. 27).

That's when Jesus said, "Do this and you will live."

So I am thinking about the word "live." Jesus did not include the modifier "eternal" in His response. He reduced the question about "eternal life" to "live," a verb instead of a noun. I think Jesus is talking about a quality of life, not just quantity, and I think He is talking about present life, not just future. "Do this and you will live" sounds very much like a prediction about what I will experience both in this life and the next should I somehow come to love God and neighbor as I should.

The blinders will come off if you do this—love God and neighbor. Your peripheral vision will be restored along with your interest in the wide world around you. And a sense of the great expanse of God's creation stretching behind you, before you, and out beyond you on all sides until it disappears from view in a circular perimeter around your tiny speck of a life, will come upon you. When your vision is fully restored, and you realize the truth of your own minuscule presence in the incomprehensible intellectual and geographic and chronological space of God's creation, you will then have the opportunity to "live."

Until the blinders come off—until your universe is centered in God rather than yourself—your life will be a weak and fleeting shadow of what it should be and what it is intended to be.

You don't really live if all you ever see are the bricks in front of your nose as you pull the buggy down the street. You have seen those bricks a thousand times before. You are just as trapped in mind and spirit as you are in space, like a mouse running on the wheel that never takes him anywhere.

Jesus said, "I have come that they may have life, and have it to the full" (John 10:10). This life "to the full" is the same as the "live" of "Do this and you will live."

The blinders only come off as the love of God and neighbor takes over.

I am sure it is frightening to have those blinders come down after years of plodding along within established mental and spiritual parameters. Disorientation might be the most common response to such a dramatic change in vision.

But we are already disoriented as humans. We plod along knowing that life is supposed to be more than this existence we endure day by day. Life—my life—has to have some meaning and purpose beyond the next paving brick. We already long for a richer, fuller life with more beauty, more truth, more goodness, and more grace. We want that life "to the full" that Jesus talked about. We want to really live.

You can get there, according to Jesus of Nazareth. Your life can be abundant, flowing like an artesian well inside of you.

The key to it all is in this famous and terse summation of all the Old Testament law and prophets: loving God and loving neighbor. And the key to loving neighbors, according to Jesus, is keeping your eyes wide open for those moments when your life intersects another life at the point of need. These intersections where our lives meet the lives of strangers are rich in their teaching and learning potential. They can be transformational. We are well advised to expect them to occur, to prepare for their occurrence, and to develop a simple strategy for how we will deal with them—like "love your neighbor as yourself."

My geographical and spiritual journey took me from Center City to New Orleans. In the process I realized that something was changing in me, and something had to change in my world.

## CARE EFFECT #3: MY NEIGHBOR IS CHANGED

We know with certainty that God is pleased and glorified when we care for others in practical deeds of kindness and love. We know this because He commanded it as the summary of all the instruction in the law and the prophets.

We know with certainty that receiving and giving care changes us. We can trace the changes in our own lives as we sort through memories and the faces of caregivers come to mind. We are certain both from the instruction of the Bible and from our own experience that we experience change.

But what about that neighbor to whom I extend my love? Will he or she really be changed by my love? We have our own personal testimony of transformation through loving care. But we also know of instances where love was given with no apparent response.

I believe that love is the most powerful force in this universe. I believe this affirmation to be true: "God is love." I believe that the absence of love in my life is a sure indication that I do not know God (see 1 John 4:8). The Spirit of God abiding in me produces the fruit of love.

Will I see a change in my neighbor if I truly extend my love?

Sometimes we come upon a situation of evident need where we have the resources to help, as in the parable of the Good Samaritan. Sometimes we only learn about the needs through a process of discovery.

People with needs live in your community. Their needs are your opportunity to share God's love and good news. When you see a person or persons in need you should routinely ask yourself if your awareness of that need is God's call to you to help.

Our church felt compelled by the Spirit of God to do more than we were doing. Promoting homeownership was our "next step" in helping our neighbors in the Ninth Ward of New Orleans. Our journey of discovery may help provide some insight for your next steps in bearing witness to the amazing love of Christ by loving your neighbor.

## CHILDREN AT HOME IN THE COLD AND DARK

The wind was cold. I tugged the coat collar tightly around my neck and pulled some Christmas presents from the trunk of the car. Janet, my wife, picked up presents as well.

The address we sought was on the "brick" side of the Florida Housing Community. These apartments would soon be demolished. The preferred homes now were on the "paint" side. These buildings were bright, colorful, and brand new.

We found the number on the building and struggled to make our way around bags of trash in the stairwell. "Who is responsible for trash pickup?" I wondered.

I found the apartment number and knocked on the door. The door swung inward, and the faces of children filled the opening. I peered into the darkness behind them. Their home had no electricity or gas to dispel the cold. All the windowpanes were broken, and the apertures were covered with plywood. Pallets lay next to the walls on bare concrete where the children slept. I could see no furniture.

First Baptist New Orleans operated a Kid's Club in the Florida Housing Community from 1991 until Katrina. I remember seeing the T-shirts for the first time and being confused, thinking that "Florida" was the state. Every Saturday a group of volunteers went to the community center playground, played games with the children, taught Bible lessons, sang songs, and fed them lunch. Sometimes rudimentary medical care was provided by medical residents and nurses. Clothing and Christmas gifts were distributed to children and adults alike.

We started that ministry in 1991, the year 17 people were murdered in that one housing community and New Orleans became the homicide capital of America. We helped families bury their teenagers shot dead in the streets. We comforted little children who tracked through the blood of murders outside their doors. We brought them to church, took them to camp by the hundreds, and placed some of them in the Louisiana Baptist Children's Home.

The Upper Ninth Ward, like most areas of high crime and poverty, was largely populated by single mothers and their children. The husbands and fathers were mostly absent, many of them dead or in prison.

The inside of this home was a dark and bare space, windowless and cold. I was reminded of homes I had visited in the *favelas* (slums) of Mexico City.

We delivered our Christmas presents, but I left that home knowing that we had not fulfilled our Christian responsibility toward those children. As a community, and as a community of faith, we were failing these little ones.

We walked away from that home, but what I saw there never left my mind and heart. We left those little ones stranded in a home that was unhealthy, unsafe, and unsavory. They would not have described it that way, of course, but they were experiencing that reality day after day and night after night.

I treasure a picture of a 10- or 12-year-old boy sitting on his bicycle beside one of the new houses we built—his house. It reminds me of the reason we launched that enormous effort in the first place—children who needed a clean and safe place to live. That boy's life was changed when he and his mother moved into their new house. As they pay their mortgage, principle only, no interest due, the mother is developing an inheritance for her son. Life has changed financially and fundamentally for their family.

That's part of the Care Effect.

## REFLECTIONS

1. How wide is the concern of Christ and His church for people who are in need?
2. Are people in your church aware of the needs in the community?
3. How would you describe the responsibility that the church of Jesus Christ has to care for the widows and orphans? What about single moms?
4. Could you modify your regular weekly path to include visits to the needy in your community?

## FUNDAMENTAL MISSIONS QUESTIONS

My visit to a remote mountain village in Papua confirmed what I had read—the Moni Tribe, along with many other peoples, received the gospel of Jesus Christ with joy. Although they continue to live in isolation, these brothers and sisters of ours are making progress both in their understanding of the gospel and in lifestyle changes that increase their health and well-being. Missionaries work on both fronts in the region. They teach the Scriptures and assist the church leaders. They also conduct medical clinics, develop kindergarten programs, build airstrips, and construct clean-water systems.

The spring water that supplied the missionary house also descended to the village itself through a system of garden hoses. Gravity alone applied sufficient water pressure for basic needs in the few public buildings.

The missionaries asked me to speak to the church members upon my arrival. Hundreds of villagers crushed into the small church building after sunset. The front rows filled with children who arrived a half hour early and sang until church began.

We ate dinner late, after church. I was tired, I remember, and ready to hit the sheets. But one of the missionaries had a question for me before we turned in. This is how I remember the ensuing, lengthy conversation.

"How do you feel about your experience so far?" she asked. Her profile flickered in the dim light of a 12-volt bulb.

"Tonight was wonderful," I said. "Those children sing like angels from heaven." They sang in their tribal language and Indonesian—no English.

"But I couldn't shake a feeling of sadness for the children," I continued. And that was really it—the sadness. I dropped my head and closed my eyes. And I saw again the outstretched hands of little children, street urchins, in the poverty-stricken places of the world.

I felt this sadness in the barren industrial slums of villages along the Mexico-United States border. Those children were bright-eyed, too, and I developed a friendship with a 12-year-old who had so many dreams. I knew as the church van pulled out of his neighborhood that none of his dreams would come true.

A pre-adolescent child in the refugee camp of Barranquilla, Colombia, struck me the same way. A brief visit in the shanty she called "home" was almost too much to endure. Suffering from sexual abuse, lacking access to educational opportunities, and living without city services, she was already buried in a world with no windows.

The missionary was a little upset at my remark. She had turned from her medical assignment after many years in Papua to focus primarily on religious instruction. "Why are you sad for the children?" she asked with an edge in her voice.

I knew in my heart that this conversation would be difficult. It has always been one of the key discussions for Christian missionaries and a point of contention.

"They have so much potential," I replied. "But they will never see it develop. They will get only a third-grade education. They have no real access to health care. They see so many of their newborns die from dysentery. They themselves are likely to die of malnutrition and preventable diseases before they reach their fortieth birthdays."

"Already their hair is turning orange," I said, staring at my hands. The orange hue was a sure sign of malnutrition.

"But why are you worried about that?" she asked, leaning forward into the circle. "They know Jesus as their Savior. They are going to heaven. And they are happy."

We were in the company of a few others. A North American pastor and his wife arrived in Papua about the same time I did. We came from different directions and had met for the first time earlier in the day. The pastor served on the missions board for his denomination. Their efforts resulted in an extensive network of churches in Indonesia, and especially in Papua.

"I think we have a responsibility to help them achieve a better quality of life," this fellow pastor commented.

"I know what David is talking about," added another missionary who had built the home where we were staying. He was a lifelong resident of the mountains of Papua and worked for years as a liaison between the giant mining operations and the native people groups that lived in the vicinity.

"I ran into a man on a trail a few days ago," he continued. "He and I grew up together as children. We were good friends, and we began to reminisce. He told me that he envied me. I asked him why. He said that I could come and go as I pleased but that he was trapped in Papua and could never leave. It's true."

Americans admired him for giving up all the privileges of citizenship to live in the primitive and harsh environs of Papua. But Papuans saw him as a prince or king, a man of means who could come and go at will. He lived in Papua when cannibalism was still widely practiced on the island, when missionaries were threatened, when Christianity was a strange and different way to think about God and the world. He also experienced the rapid advance of the gospel of Christ in Papua when whole tribes adopted the Bible as their guide, the church as their house of worship, and Christ as their Savior.

Missions boards struggle with the tension between older missions fields that need continuing support and new fields where the name of Christ is not even known. Some boards refuse to fund missionaries who remain in the older fields, preferring to send them where the gospel is not yet known. Papua is now considered an older field, and missions support from some sources is in decline.

The pastor who served on his group's missions board articulated his own view that quality of life issues were germane to the missions discussion. He felt that their missionaries should remain in Papua teaching the people and assisting them with the development of nutrition and education as well as their spiritual lives.

Given the limited resources available for the support of missionaries around the world, some consider it a moral obligation to target people groups who have never heard the gospel. Others believe that missionaries should remain longer and address both fuller understanding of the gospel and issues like nutrition, clean water, medicine, and education. We talked into the night about these things, two pastors from the western world and two long-tenured missionaries immersed in the stone-age culture of remote Papuan villages.

My own view is this: the gospel presentation is not completed while the convert is still lying in the ditch. We who speak the good news must incarnate the good news through loving deeds. Until the good news addresses the pain of hunger, malnutrition, and preventable diseases, our evangelism ("evangel" means good news) is not done. The Good Samaritan might have bandaged the man's wounds and left him in the ditch. He might have carried him to the inn and spent the rest of his money on others in crisis. Instead, he saw the injured man as his neighbor in need and made an astonishing investment in his well-being.

The gospel is most powerful in this kind of world when it is coupled with, not separated from, deeds of kindness that announce and explain the love of God to neighbors in need. Nurturing new work toward fuller health spiritually and physically is a more effective evangelistic strategy. Establishing medical clinics, schools, and other similar work and institutions should be hardwired to planting churches in every culture, especially one so in need as in Papua. The Gospel writer observed that Jesus "grew in wisdom and stature, and in favor with God and man" (Luke 2:52). Our missions work will grow in the same way, including finding favor with human authority, if we will continue to present and implement the totality of the "good news" that both saves the soul and binds the wounds of our neighbor.

## REFLECTIONS

1. If a child loves Jesus and is going to go to heaven when she dies, does it really matter if she dies at 40 or 80 years of age? Why or why not?

2. Does it really matter to you if you die at 40 or 80? Why or why not?

3. What responsibility has the church of Jesus Christ, if any, to address hunger and malnutrition in your community and/or the world?

4. Is the gospel presented more winsomely with an intentional focus on caring for neighbors in need?

## THE HALF-LIFE OF SIMPLE KINDNESS

Have you ever contemplated the lasting impact of giving a Bible to a newborn?

I grabbed my guitar by the neck and swung it out of the back seat, turning as I did to scan the apartment complex for some sign of the clubhouse. The unpleasant twang of tortured strings brought my attention back to the guitar, but not before I located the pool with its iron fence and blue water. Taking more care now, I checked the guitar for scrapes and closed the car door.

Having marched through this routine a hundred times before in other places, I felt only slightly self-conscious walking through the lobby with a Bible in one hand and a guitar in the other. A guitar always rouses curiosity, I have discovered, and people will smile and say, "Going to play something for us?"

I had scarcely surveyed the clubhouse and chosen a likely corner for our first meeting before Eric arrived. He quickly found the cookies and the cold drinks that the apartment management was providing for the Bible study. We set up and waited for two o'clock.

One elderly lady walked in promptly at the hour. As we introduced ourselves, Agnes said she didn't do much singing, so I left the guitar in its leaning position against the wall. At the prayer time, she mentioned her grandson in the Middle East on the USS *Eisenhower*.

We opened our Bibles for the study time, and Agnes, who appeared to be about 70 years old, pulled out a weathered pocket New Testament. It appeared to be one like the Gideons distribute, and I quizzed her to discover the story behind it.

The Bible, she said, was decades old, and she didn't really know why she still had it. She had thought about getting rid of it but had kept it instead for its sentimental value.

She handed it to me and continued to talk. I opened the front cover and read these words, *Presented to Richard Larry Dowell by Fidelis Class, South Main Baptist Church, Houston, Texas, January 3, 1947.*

"Who was Richard?" I asked.

"He was my youngest boy," she said. Her eyes grew wet with tears. "He died of cancer when he was 11 years old. He was sick for six months." We waited for her voice and eyes to clear so she could go on.

"We were attending South Main at the time," she said, and wiped her eyes again.

"This Fidelis Class gave him the Bible January 3," I said, but she corrected me.

"No, that was Richard's birthday."

"Oh, so the class gave him a Bible to commemorate his birth."

"That's right," she said. Agnes went on to tell us about her family, which consisted of four boys and four girls. She and her husband had not attended church for some time.

We held that meeting three or four times, and only Agnes came. She told us that we could spend our time reaching more people, and we finally abandoned the effort.

That pocket New Testament is hard to forget. The young married couple received it for their baby and kept it when he died. They watched their other children grow up and leave home and finally found themselves alone in an apartment in Southwest Houston, a little afraid to get out too much, tentative about church attendance. The gift Bible, however, survived the years and stayed with them when the children were gone and church had ceased to be a weekly routine.

If wrinkled hands could speak they would tell of untold hours of folding and ironing, washing and drying, changing diapers and dressing children. The story of her life was written somewhere in Agnes's aging hands.

If that little New Testament could speak, it would also have a story to tell—of a Sunday School class of older women that cared enough to provide Bibles for the newborns in the church. It would tell of busy hands that plucked it from the shelves and opened its cover to write a little boy's name inside—probably a little boy the hands had never touched, maybe never would.

The little Bible would tell of a journey through the nursery at South Main Baptist Church, of a Sunday School worker presenting it to a new mother with a baby in her arms, saying something like, "This is for little Richard. We are glad to give him his first Bible."

Richard kept the Bible until he died. I suppose that he read it, perhaps regularly, even at his age, and especially in his illness. And when he died, his mother couldn't part with that Bible, though it was getting yellow with age even then.

Some day—maybe many days—you will perform some simple act of love and think nothing about it, and that act of love will be the stack pole of a person's walk with God. That act of love will survive the years when other things are dropped and gone, and a gray-headed saint will bow in prayer, remember what you did years ago, and thank God for you.

The half-life of an act of kindness may be a thousand years. You never know when you are walking, not in sand, but in wet cement.

## REFLECTIONS

1. What acts of kindness are routine in the systematic ministries of your church?
2. How did these compassionate works become an integral part of your church and its ministries?
3. Can you think of an act of kindness that some did for you that some people might have been considered small but meant a lot to you?

## CARE EFFECT #4: MY WORLD IS CHANGED

Following Jesus is a radical thing to do. Jesus did not simply conform to social or political customs. He lived beyond artificial norms and operated in the realm of divine truth. We, His followers, have an opportunity to do just that. But we, too, must be able to identify and discard the unholy norms that are stumbling blocks rather than stepping stones. And we must be able to reorient our lives around the kingdom of God and its reconfiguration of all seams and connections.

The world mission of the church affords the followers of Jesus a unique perspective and opportunity in the global discussion. We are not trying to conquer kingdoms or topple armies. This is not our mission in the world. We are seeking to represent the One whose very presence is peace. We are inviting people to the Lord's Table.

Deeds of compassion have amazing effects within groups— familial, cultural, social, and ethnic. We witness this within small groups more easily than large groups. A small group will adjust its vocabulary and activities to accommodate a member whose loving concern is connected to faith in Christ. Consistent, passionate, and surprising acts of love are strong enough to transform the dynamics of group relationships.

We do not yet know the full extent of love's transforming power. We know that God's love changes us. We know that the love of a mother or father or spouse changes us. But we have not yet realized or internalized the amazing potential of love unleashed in larger social connections.

Your family dynamics will change through the power of love embodied in deeds. Your church will transform as well. Your community will take note of your love when they see your church, not as a destination, but as a force for compassion and healing.

There is so much cynicism and skepticism in our world. I shared the story of salvation through Christ with a young woman as we walked together one day. When I told her that God loved her, she said, "Why would God love me? No one has ever loved me."

A woman became connected to our church through our compassion ministries. She observed us for a time, and then she told me her story. At 12 years of age her parents left her beside a Dumpster in Las Vegas. They told her they would be right back to pick her up. They never returned.

Multitudes around us feel like they are discarded trash sitting by a Dumpster waiting for the hearse to pick them up. They have no sense of their own value or the value of others. They are empty and angry.

They open fire on a world that they feel kicks them aside and leaves them in the dust.

How do we reach a world so turned against itself?

We reach this kind of world with love. "God so loved the world that he gave" (John 3:16). We must love this world enough to give, not just a cracker or a cup or a word of advice, but ourselves.

When we love enough to give ourselves, people will be surprised. We will get their attention. The Apostle Peter said that if we lived in practical ways with Christ as Lord we would stir up the curiosity of a watching world. "Always be prepared to give an answer to everyone who asks you to give the reason for the hope that you have" (1 Peter 3:15). People are bound to be surprised by a love that motivates us to lay down our lives and take up the towel and serve.

Deeds of love and compassion, offered in the name of our crucified Lord, are like seeds sown in the earth. At the proper time they will bear fruit even in this kind of world (see Galatians 6:9).

## JESUS AND THE LAW OF LOVE

Jesus fulfilled the law, He did not abolish it (Matthew 5:17). But His fulfillment of it is a radical distillation and condensation of all that the law required into the simple but difficult law of love—the "royal law," as James called it (James 2:8).

Jesus knows that the moral or ceremonial law of the Old Testament will not cleanse us or make us powerful. It will not. Instead, He gives us a new commandment that is sufficient in itself to restrict bad behavior and inspire good behavior. Love alone has the flexibility and rigidity necessary to guide the disciples of Jesus in every age and every place.

The law of love is governed by the need of the neighbor. We learn this both in the teaching and the living of Jesus. He responds to need throughout His ministry. He heals all who were oppressed by the devil. He healed all the sick. When confronted with human hurt and need, Jesus acted to heal it.

He taught us that love of neighbor is like responding to the need of a man beaten and robbed and left half-dead by the side of the road. This complicated example of caring for another human being shows how the need of the neighbor shapes the loving response of the disciple.

The church has been most effective in changing its world when it has followed the example and teaching of Christ in laying down His life for His friends. The radical call of Jesus to love your neighbor, to love your enemy, and to do good to those who persecute you is the key to world transformation by the church.

Our community of faith will only transform New Orleans as we practice this kind of self-giving love. No other force on earth is powerful enough to change human hearts, behavior, and society.

Jesus discusses this peculiar quality that He hopes will be displayed in His disciples. He wants them to be meek and lowly, pure in heart and peace-makers. All of these are qualities of the life of love.

Jesus wants His disciples to guard their hearts. He teaches us to identify sin in its birthplace—the heart. We are to be perfect as the Father in heaven is perfect, eliminating greed and lust and hatred from our hearts. The pure in heart will see God.

We must remember that we are doing something very unusual here. We are organizing our behavior and attitudes on the foundation of the person and work of Jesus Christ. This is what distinguishes us as the church in the world. People outside of faith in Christ will find this approach strange and unwarranted. But we believe that Jesus is the way, the truth, and the life.

Therefore, we are compelled to heed and obey.

The way of love is risky. Ultimately it cost Jesus His life, and this has been true for many of His faithful followers. Other lesser risks are just as real, including the risk of rejection, persecution, and abandonment.

Disciples of Jesus have been willing to take these risks in order to faithfully live the life of self-giving love. In so doing they have surprised and disturbed the world, challenged its assumptions, turned commonly accepted truths inside out, and forced families, communities, and even nations to acknowledge and address needs and injustices that would otherwise have gone unchanged.

## REFLECTIONS

1. Are you taking any risks as a Christian? What are they?
2. Have you felt called to do something for Christ that you have not yet done? What is preventing you from going forward?
3. What does it mean to lay down our lives for the sake of the gospel?

## THE TUSSLE WITH THE TABLE

The Lord Jesus instituted the ordinance of communion and in so doing sentenced members of His church to a constant tussle with the table both physically and spiritually. We know it is the Lord's Table, not ours. The Lord Himself serves us at this table. The Lord Himself sends out invitations to the table. He controls the dinner list, not us. In fact, He sends us into the highways and hedges passing out the invitations to whomever will hear and come.

This is the great world mission of the church. Everyone who believes in Jesus is part of this world mission. We are called to see the world, not just our little spot in it. And we are called to have the people of the world in our minds and in our prayers.

The symbol of the table stays upon our hearts as followers of Jesus. We know that we do not deserve to be served at this table, that nothing we have done has earned us a place. Every time we receive the bread and the cup we are chagrined by our poor performance and cast back upon the sheer grace of it all. We cannot plumb this mystery—that we have a place at the Lord's Table. It is too deep for reason, logic, or any human wisdom.

I sit down in one of the chairs and slide my hand across the smooth wooden surface of the table. I touch the space beside me at the table. I do not control who will sit in that space at my elbow passing me the bread. Jesus Himself is the true host at this table, and He may invite anyone He chooses to sit beside me at His table. In fact, if I come to the Lord's Table, I do so surrendering all of my rights. He is the host;

I am the guest. I will eat what He provides. I will sit where He places me. I will dress as He instructs me—black tie or business casual. If I refuse the instructions of the host, He may refuse to seat me at His table.

Jesus loves and cares for sinners—all those people we might judge to be below us. We might suppose we are among the beautiful people in the world, those with proper training, superior appearance, and elevated social standing.

We are continually tempted to organize our social world in these layers because we are sinners and unable to know or embrace the Father's true nature. This sense of our superiority among the humans on the planet is the deepest lie we have ever been told or accepted. It is the lie that drops down the steel curtain between us and God. Nothing so offends the Father as the arrogance of heart that elevates a vile sinner and relegates one of the Father's loved ones to second-class status.

The Father attacks these false rankings at the table. He insists not only that you serve the person to your right and left at the table, He also insists that you receive their service as well. This is how the table works. And this is what it means to sit at the table where someone else, not you, is the host. If you want a place at the Lord's table, prepare to eat with those who have been prostitutes and tax collectors. If you cannot stomach such a thing, don't come to the table. In refusing the invitation to such a table, you may think yourself too good for the company. Actually, however, you reckon yourself unworthy of the grace of God.

## REFLECTIONS

1. How do you feel about this picture of God as a waiter at the table?
2. What about the Lord's Table in your church? What does it symbolize for you?
3. Is the ground really level at the Cross? Is it level in our own social thinking?

## HOMOGENEOUS MEALTIME

*I was picking through my own plate, trying to find something I could eat without any reservation, when I heard a loud crunching sound right behind me. I turned to find the host of the meal, a business man in this small Peruvian town, gripping a fried* cuy *(Spanish for guinea pig) in his hand as he walked around the table. The crunching sound I heard was the sound of his teeth breaking through the skull to get to those delicious fried* cuy *brains.*

We are all uneasy with this conversation. Homogeneity in the church of Jesus Christ seems inevitable, yet it also seems off. We know that it doesn't fit our mental picture of the heavenly gathering where people from every nation, tribe, and tongue are assembled together.

The principle of homogeneity is deeply embedded in our understanding of human interaction and especially our experience at the dinner table. It seems incontrovertible and indisputable: humans gather with their own kind. The gospel travels along family and friendship lines. These are the "bridges of God," as Donald McGavran helped us understand in his seminal work, *Bridges of God*, first published in 1954. Its publication was the beginning of what has been called the "church growth movement." His book was not necessarily a recommendation that the church of Jesus Christ around the world divide up according to ethnicity and economic standing, it was an observation that the church around the world and throughout generations has done so. He also observed that churches grow faster in all cultures where they gather in homogeneous groups (also see McGavran's book *How Churches Grow*).

By gathering in homogeneous groups we feel we are removing an unnecessary barrier for someone who is contemplating coming to Christ. Ethnic and cultural barriers are so powerful that people will refuse to come to Christ if they know that it means sitting at the table with someone from a group of people whom they loathe—a Jew with a Gentile, for instance.

Jesus could certainly have configured His church this way from the beginning. He could have insisted that different congregations be established for different ethnic groups. In the first century this would have meant that Jews met at one place for worship and Gentiles met at another. Was it really necessary that Jews and Gentiles gather in the same congregation? Was it necessary for the sake of the gospel message?

The idea that we should gather at the Lord's Table in homogeneous groups, groups of people who are socially and culturally compatible, is the very opposite of what Jesus is doing at His table. It makes sense only if you are structuring the Lord's Table as if it were exactly like any other human gathering. But Jesus destroyed the barrier between Jew and Gentile, slave and free, white and black, rich and poor. He made the two one in His death upon the Cross. He made peace between the warring factions. He launched the solitary gathering among humans where the homogeneous rule does not and cannot apply—His church. Here we are one in Christ Jesus. That must be the end of it because this is His table, not ours.

I think we lose something essential to the gospel when our churches are divided up along cultural and social lines. Our gospel presentation is warped, misshapen. It lacks the startling love of neighbor that was obvious in the words and deeds of Jesus and should be obvious in His church.

A church conformed to the world in this way cannot speak with authority to the injustices that are always part of such divisions. The church of Jesus Christ around the world cannot represent her Lord faithfully while displaying and defending such divisions. Ethnic hatred, violence, and injustice rage in every corner of our globe, and the church is often immobilized and even complicit in such acts because she looks like the world instead of like heaven.

People do gravitate toward their own kind. This may be observed in any human interaction. "Gravitate" means "to sink or settle, fall or descend." It is the natural process whereby heavier objects drop to the bottom and lighter ones rise to the top, sorted by gravity. The church of Jesus Christ will gravitate if we let it. Our own hearts will do the same. We will gravitate to people exactly like us unless we deliberately choose another course.

When you come to the Lord's Table, you are deliberately choosing another course. Jesus was noteworthy in that He did not "show partiality" (Luke 20:21). Peter learned at the home of Cornelius, "I now realize how true it is that God does not show favoritism" (Acts 10:34). These are the footsteps we follow.

All human societies have their own versions of the Jew-Gentile cultural groups that despise one another. If a church anywhere at any time should defend the exclusion of certain followers of Jesus based solely upon ethnicity or cultural barriers, then that gathering has forfeited the right to call itself "Christian." This is made perfectly clear in Ephesians 2:14–18:

> *For he himself is our peace, who has made the two groups one and has destroyed the barrier, the dividing wall of hostility, by setting aside in his flesh the law with its commands and regulations. His purpose was to create in himself one new humanity out of the two, thus making peace, and in one body to reconcile both of them to God through the cross, by which he put to death their hostility. He came and preached peace to you who were far away and peace to those who were near. For through him we both have access to the Father by one Spirit.*

The world has never been more in need of Christ's church and its testimony both in word and action to the destruction of these cultural and ethnic barriers. We must begin to see such inclusiveness and diversity in the body of Christ as essential to the gospel rather than ancillary to it. As we recover the true nature of Christ's mealtime, we will represent our Lord more fully. Our gospel proclamation will be empowered because the church actually looks like heaven, the way it is supposed to look, as we all know. And the good news of Jesus Christ will no longer be distorted by a tolerance for or even advocacy of these racial, ethnic, and cultural divides that our Father in Heaven refuses to tolerate at His table.

## BRINGING DOWN THE BARRIERS

Caring for neighbors who are hurting or in need is one sure way of bringing down the artificial barriers that divide people. Our regular paths to school and work may not take us by the poor and neglected people in our community. But our works of compassion will certainly do this. They create for us a regular appointment outside of our own cultural bubble. As we begin to go to the prison or nursing home—the highways and hedges—we may discover that this moment is often the richest and most rewarding moment of our day or week. We go intending to serve, and we ourselves are served in the process.

Deeds of compassion deliberately designed for easy access and participation by church members will foster understanding and friendship across the barriers. Maybe immediately, but at least eventually, these bonds of love will result in a communion of saints that more fully reflects the gathering in heaven we will experience one day.

This is not heaven yet. Sin is still present with us and still present in Christ's church. The inevitable is bound to happen. Yet we can be prophets in our own day, attacking the divisions that undercut the gospel everywhere in the world. Perhaps the most effective way we can do this in our churches is through compassion ministries that reach out across the social and cultural divides. When we do this, we will end up serving one another at the same table.

While working on this book, a seminary student confided in me. He had gone to talk with a pastor search committee. That committee asked him about "multi-culturalism." He said something like this: "I am glad you brought that up. I want you to know that I believe the church is open to all people in the community."

That was the end of his candidacy in that particular church. They were not interested in people from various cultures gathering in their worship service.

I am sure there is a way to nuance this position either through church growth theory or another method where it seems more palatable and less racist. But it doesn't sound like Jesus to me. And it doesn't sound like the early church where Jew and Gentile were called to worship together despite the discomfort for both groups. If it doesn't look and sound like Jesus and the Book of Acts, what might this church, intentionally and adamantly mono-cultural, resemble?

Jesus was intent on caring for all people regardless of race or economic class. His church should be intent on reaching all people and adamant that we do not discriminate based on race or social standing. If we fail to bring down these barriers in our churches, we betray our Lord and pervert our presentation of the gospel.

## JESUS PLAYED THE RACE CARD

Jesus himself played the race card in His most famous story. At first I thought that He did so without any necessity but for dramatic effect. He was answering the question, "Who is my neighbor?" His story answered that question by addressing the perennial, perpetual, and universal issue of ethnic divisions among humans. According to Jesus, loving our neighbor necessarily involves crossing these great divides among us. This does not happen in the way we expect, however—we, the greater and gracious, serving them, the lesser and needy. The Good Samaritan represents a despised ethnic group. But he is the one who loves across the barrier, not vice versa. The Jew who asked the question is startled to learn that he must receive love and service from Samaritans as part of the Great Commandment. It is he, the expert in the law, who lies wounded and needy in the ditch.

Oh, this Jesus, He makes me crazy! He sits me down at His table and makes me receive the bread and the cup from a Samaritan!

## REFLECTIONS

1. Have you ever eaten a meal where you were extremely uncomfortable and afraid of the food?
2. Are you disturbed or angry about this discussion? Please explain.
3. Can you think of a church in the New Testament that was established only for one ethnic group? Why or why not?

4. How would it have been easier if, from the first, Jews had gathered in Jewish churches and Gentiles had gathered in Gentile churches? Why didn't they do this?

5. You want to change your world. You think that your faith in Christ is the key. You want to make the good news of God's love known everywhere. Can you think of a more startling display of love than the cross-cultural rescue from the roadside of your sworn enemy? Could this be the strategy that Jesus' love requires and that a world like this one needs?

# PART FOUR

# Do Not Give Up on Good

*Let us not become weary in doing good,
for at the proper time we will reap a harvest
if we do not give up. Therefore, as we have
opportunity, let us do good to all people,
especially to those who belong to the
family of believers.*

GALATIANS 6:9–10


*Make every effort to add to your faith goodness.*

2 PETER 1:5


*I remain confident of this: I will see the goodness
of the LORD in the land of the living.*

PSALM 27:13

WE BELIEVE THAT GOD IS GOOD, THAT GOD IS LOVE. GOD is the Creator of this universe. His divine nature is the core truth of all that there is. Our confession of faith is this: "Surely your goodness and love will follow me all the days of my life" (Psalm 23:6).

If God is not good, then we are all lost forever. The goodness of God is fundamental to our faith.

Our efforts to do good to all are a confession of faith. We believe that good wins over evil. We believe that we should return evil with good.

As I type these lines the sun has not yet risen. The clouds are overcast. A light mist blankets New Orleans. I opened a kitchen window slightly, and the predawn morning is peppered with intermittent rain.

And someone is crying. I can hear the whimpers through my open window.

The world is truly full of pain. Open the window, and you will hear. The Old Testament word translated "flesh" refers to man's frailty, weakness, and need. Our survival depends upon access to things such as food, water, and air. We are needy. Lacking the necessities of life, we live in pain.

God comes to us in our need. Often He comes through people. "But God, who comforts the downcast, comforted us by the coming of Titus" (2 Corinthians 7:6). Titus was the very presence and heart of God to Paul in his need.

## NO ONE (ELSE) IS COMING

When New Orleans needed a helping hand out of the mess we were in, God's people showed up to help. Some people came who had no faith, of course. But the vast majority of those who came were people motivated by their faith in Christ.

I have gone into prisons hundreds of times throughout the years. I find that volunteers in prisons are almost universally motivated by their faith. For most of them, they hear the words of Jesus, "I was in prison and you came to visit me," and they go (see Matthew 25:36).

Visiting with the residents of Rivarde Juvenile Detention Center is one of our community ministries. We usually find about 30 juveniles living in the five pods. These youth are at great risk. The guard house wall is papered with hundreds of obituaries of former residents at Rivarde who have been killed on the streets of New Orleans.

We pray before we enter and ask God to help us as we teach Scripture and talk with the young people. The corridors are long in prison, and the gates clang loudly when they shut. Prisons are bleak and full of hard surfaces. The juvenile detention center is a prison.

During one visit, I sat down at a table and began to talk to the boys, reading Scripture and applying it to their lives as best I could. I thought I was doing pretty well when one of the boys, maybe 15 years old, looked right at me and asked, "What are you doing here?"

The question startled me. I scrambled for an answer. "I just want to read some Scripture and pray with you."

He repeated the question: "What are you doing here?" Then he added: "No one comes to see us. Why are you here?"

I took the opportunity to talk about the love of Christ for me. "Jesus commands us to love others," I said. "That's why I am here."

The young man had this curious look on his face, puzzled and amazed. He shook his head slightly, and then he said, "Thank you. No one comes to see us."

Some might call this the "ministry of presence."

The point is this: no one else is coming. Any assumption that surely someone is coming is wrong.

No one is coming.

Human beings languish in prisons and nursing homes and dark corners of the earth.

And no one is coming to express love and concern for the fearful and lonely and broken—just disciples of Jesus like you, motivated by faith and love. The young man in prison was not hanging on every word I spoke. He was not even hearing my words at that moment. My presence alone in that prison was so loud a word it drowned out everything else I said. He was stunned, captivated, and confused, seeing me there with him in his incarceration. He literally had no idea why I would show up.

## REFLECTIONS

1. Do you know about the "ministry of presence"? How so?
2. Have persons motivated only by humanitarian concerns, not faith, ever ministered to you? If so, when and how?
3. Tell about one experience of ministry where your presence was the main event, not your words.

# NO NEED FOR THANK YOU

*And I will very gladly spend and be spent for your souls; though the more abundantly I love you, the less I am loved.*

—2 CORINTHIANS 12:15 (KJV)

Reading the Apostle Paul's second letter to Corinth is like putting your hand over his beating heart. He held nothing back as he honestly and passionately expressed his love and frustration with these friends.

*I robbed other churches by receiving support from them so as to serve you. And when I was with you and needed something, I was not a burden to anyone.*

—2 CORINTHIANS 11:8–9

The great apostle carried the gospel of life to these in need, yet they did not return his kindness as would have been right and honorable. Instead, they criticized him, belittled him, and compared him in unkind ways with other preachers they deemed more admirable.

The apostle wrote this second letter as a third attempt to mend the bruised relationship.

The problem with caring for others is that they may not care for you. Often they will not care for you either with the same devotion or the same attention that you exercise toward them.

Jesus healed ten lepers, lifting them out of their sickness and exile into a new life. Only one bothered to return to express his gratitude. Jesus expressed disappointment at the nine who failed to give thanks. Caregivers could be working on a 10 percent rule—10 percent of those you bless will return to bless you.

If we do our work in order that we might receive the accolades of others, then we are wrongly motivated. Jesus said plainly, "When you give to the needy, do not announce it with trumpets, as the hypocrites do in the synagogues and on the streets, to be honored by others. Truly I tell you, they have received their reward in full" (Matthew 6:2). He repeated this warning in connection with our prayers and fasting. We are not to do our devotions or our good works "to be honored by others." This would include those persons who are the immediate beneficiaries of our works of compassion.

Gratitude is not our natural state. From infancy we loudly demand what we desire, and we expect to get it. When we do not, we are angry, frustrated, and confused. Only gradually and through the deliberate instruction of people who love us do we learn to say "thank you" for benefits received. Sometimes the lesson is hard to learn.

Works of compassion offered in the name of Jesus do not depend on the gratitude of those who receive care. We feed hundreds of homeless and hungry neighbors each week. Most of them are grateful for the good food they receive. Yet some of them demand more than we offer. Some condemn us for refusing to give them money for other needs they might have.

You cannot depend on any honor being conferred by fellow human beings for your good work. And you should not pursue it. The reward we seek is the Father in heaven. Any accolades given for our good work we deflect to the Father. We want others to see our good works, yes, and then to glorify the Father in heaven.

How do we stay motivated to love our neighbor as the Good Samaritan story commands when so often those we love do not love us back? How do we keep at bay the temptation toward cynicism and unbelief in our own hearts?

First, we always seek our reward from God Himself, not from people. Our loving deeds are not motivated by the return we receive from grateful people even though sometimes that return is great. We are motivated by our love for Christ and our obedience to His Word. The power to bless others comes from Christ, and from Him we receive the blessing of the giver.

Second, we operate in faith as we do our good works. "The only thing that counts is faith expressing itself through love," the Apostle Paul wrote (Galatians 5:6). Our acts of compassion are always expressions of faith—faith in God, faith in the truth of the gospel, and faith in the power of love. We do not continually demand evidence of the efficacy of our work. We just believe that, whether those lepers return to give thanks or not, the act of love bears fruit in every life. The expression of God's love is its own reward, and it is complete in itself.

Third, we seek always to link our good deeds to clear witness for Christ. We are not simply "do-gooders" whose only offering is immediate relief. We are followers of Jesus Christ. He was famous for healing the sick and speaking the good news. We want to be known for these same dual tasks—doing love and speaking the gospel.

The act of kindness may be received flippantly or taken for granted, but it will plant a seed. That seed is best germinated and nourished in the soil of a clear witness. When we connect our cup of water to proclamation of the living water, we communicate a powerful and compelling truth. We give a three-dimensional witness, touching the eye, the ear, and the heart. Jesus is our greatest example of this strategy. Having fed the 5,000, He told them, "I am the bread of life" (John 6:35). Having healed the blind man He testified, "I am the light of the world" (John 9:5). The deeds of compassion are indicators of Jesus' true identity, that He is one with the Father.

We are always satisfied in our caring when we are careful how we live and are "making the most of every opportunity" (Ephesians 5:16).

Fourth, we remain inspired by the Lord Jesus who loved us when we did not love Him, who cared for us when we did not care for Him, and who continues to love us more than we can possibly love Him. Jesus is the premier example of the caregiver who never receives back as much as He gives.

The prophet Isaiah said of the servant of the Lord, "A bruised reed he will not break, and a smoldering wick he will not snuff out. In faithfulness he will bring forth justice; he will not falter or be discouraged till he establishes justice on earth" (Isaiah 42:3–4). We must follow Jesus in resisting discouragement, which often creeps over those who seek to do good. Jesus stayed at His task until He could say, "It is finished" (John 19:30).

The writer of Hebrews urges us to look to Jesus when we are weary or considering giving up. "Consider him who endured such opposition from sinners, so that you will not grow weary and lose heart" (Hebrews 12:3).

*"This is the way; walk in it."*

—ISAIAH 30:21

## REFLECTIONS

1. How did Jesus feel about those nine lepers who did not give thanks?
2. Do you think Jesus did His good deeds in order to hear the appreciation of the recipients?
3. How important is it for you to hear "thank you" when you do something kind?
4. Would you keep doing a ministry if you never heard the recipients express gratitude?

## YOUR CHARITY IS NOT TOXIC

True love is never toxic. The very idea of toxic love attacks the foundation of Christian ethics and the central truth of human existence. While we need to heed the warning that is couched in this language of what author Robert Lupton refers to as "toxic charity," we also need the reassurance that our good deeds, offered in love, are not wasted or harmful.

The word *charity* was used for many years to translate the Greek word *agape* as in the original King James Version of the "love chapter," 1 Corinthians 13. While modern translations now consistently translate *agape* as "love," the ancient practice points out that true charity is intertwined with genuine love. In fact, the Latin root of the word *charity* simply means "dearness" or "Christian love" (Merriam-Webster). This root focuses on the condition of the heart of the giver and contemplates nothing about the one who receives.

*Agape* is one-way, unconditional love—love that depends only on the lover, not the object of that love. *Agape* requires no response to continue. Thus people in the church will sometimes say, "I love you, and there is nothing you can do about it."

This virtue of unconditional, indestructible love seeks to follow the lead of the Creator God who loved us first, loved us best, and loved us in this way. Love is the pervasive virtue of the divine nature. As the Apostle John summarized, "God is love" (1 John 4:8, 16). This kind of love is a grace gift. All forms of grace are by definition undeserved and unearned or they are not grace.

One-way charity, then, is the only kind that exists. If I expect something in return for my supposed "charity," that is not charity at all but an economic exchange.

Robert Lupton's point is a good one. Our efforts at social activism may indeed harm the recipients instead of helping them. By definition, though, these deeds would not qualify as true charity. "Love does no harm to a neighbor," the Apostle Paul observed (Romans 13:10).

Maybe this is just semantics. But the last thing we need is another excuse to stop loving our neighbor. The end result is likely the justification of evil attitudes and motives that were never true charity in the first place.

Any giving out of our excess alone is likely to be self-serving rather than loving. These tiny forays we take to gawk at humans in painful need are not charitable. They are ugly, and always have been.

The only way to love as God has loved us is way too expensive to contemplate—the permanent abandonment of our high and mighty position to immerse ourselves in the hurt of this world. But if we follow the footsteps of Jesus, that is just where we will end up—bending over the fallen, binding up their wounds, spending our lives on behalf of others.

Things get complicated when we seek to help. The man who appears to be hurt, lying in the ditch, could be faking it. His wounds may be too deep for our skill, his need too great for our resources. We may be hurting instead of helping, giving him false hope or a momentary reprieve from a life destined for more pain and poverty.

So we will walk by on the other side of the road, as our self-centered nature instructs us to do every time. All we ever needed to salve our troubled conscience was the justification of a little creative economics.

Perhaps, however, talking about "toxic charity" will reveal the genuine nature of our love and move us to a deeper level of caring. Perhaps we will seek to give of ourselves more fully so that the healing power of love may be more fully known.

The most common toxicity in the human heart has nothing to do with charity. It is all about greed, pride, and sloth. These are the vices that make our presence toxic every time no matter what we are trying to do or who we are trying to do it with.

The strength and wisdom you need to do the right thing will come to you as you stay in loving motion toward the hurting and desperate. This work of charity is known best, not from a distance, but from the inside, not from the heights but from the depths.

This is a call to all who seek to love—wise up and re-enlist. Love never fails.

## BUT MY GIFTS ARE MISUSED

*Every good and perfect gift is from above, coming down from the Father of the heavenly lights, who does not change like shifting shadows.*

—JAMES 1:17

We misuse God's good gifts. The Bible actually has a word for the twisting of the good—"iniquity." God does not prevent the squandering or evil use of His good gifts.

God continues to give to us despite our misuse of His good gifts. In fact, we are surrounded every day by the good gifts of God who provides all things for us to enjoy.

I cannot fathom this amazing grace of God though I experience it every day. I "wonder how he could love me, a sinner, condemned, unclean" (from the hymn "I Stand Amazed in the Presence" by Charles Gabriel).

I have discovered this kind of undeserved love to be the greatest and most powerful force in my life. God sends His refreshing rain on the just and on the unjust, as Jesus said. This truth about God compels us to love our enemies and do good even to those who do evil toward us (Matthew 5:45). In fact, the good giving of God to unjust people is a core teaching of Christ and the Bible.

Sometimes I imagine myself a deserving recipient of God's amazing grace, and I sense my own generosity withering like paper in a furnace of pride. Those in need around me I imagine as less deserving than myself. I find no good reason to transfer my hard-earned and well-deserved resources to those around me with such glaring moral failings.

I want to follow in the footsteps of the divine Giver, but I hesitate in fear that my own good gifts will be wasted or misused. Acts of charity sometimes appear to be counter-productive.

My shock was indescribable the first time I saw a recipient of my own benevolence spend the money I gave him on a bottle of liquor at the corner grocery store. I drove by and glanced at someone sitting on the curb, and it was him. And he was tipping that bottle up to drink!

We serve hundreds of hot meals to the homeless and hungry each week. One evening I was helping at a feeding station, visiting with those who came. A middle-aged man approached me and began to talk. His breath and clothing wreaked of alcohol, and he was struggling to stay upright. He told me that he was addicted to alcohol and drugs.

"How in the world can you afford to buy this stuff?" I asked, truly amazed.

"I'll show you," he said, and he reached into his back pocket and pulled out a small piece of cardboard. He unfolded it for me to read. He had scrawled these words in big letters: "Hungry. Please help."

"This is how I buy my drugs and alcohol," he told me, and he thrust the cardboard back in his pocket.

How can I give my hard-earned money and time in this environment of uncertainty and sin?

Love is tough as well as tender. All parents experience this truth. All human giving occurs from one needy person to the other. The needs of the giver may skew the giving so that it harms rather than helps. This is no fault of love. This is just more evidence of the caregiver's limitations and needs.

The gift of good intention may be misused through the moral failings or limited understanding of the recipient. No caregiver can be absolutely certain that their expression of love will not be twisted for some evil purpose.

We do not escape this potential moral failure by giving to institutions. Individuals and institutions alike are susceptible to the temptations of greed and sloth.

I myself am comforted by the moral accountability of the recipients of charity. The giver of the gift is a moral partner with the recipient. I feel both sides of this responsibility as the pastor of my church. I will give an account on judgment day of my own generosity or lack thereof. I will also give an account of how I used the gifts of others.

The act of charity involves two parties, and each has their own unique opportunity and responsibility. Neither one can be held morally accountable for the other.

The closer the gift is to my own hand and eyes the more likely I am to evaluate correctly the impact of my gift. If I give my money where my hands are working, I know with some measure of comfort what my gift will do. We encourage our working volunteers to support with their money what they support with their time and energy.

Sometimes we feel compelled to respond to urgent needs far away. But we should always request—and even require—minimal financial accountability from those institutions we support including budgets, financial statements, and financial endorsement by watchdog groups (e.g., the seal of the Evangelical Council for Financial Accountability).

## REFLECTIONS

1. Try to remember a time when somebody meant to help you but only made things worse. Would this be toxic charity?
2. Are you doing something right now, ostensibly out of love, that is really hurting the one you say you love?
3. Could you change your approach to someone you are now helping in a way that would empower rather than creating a dependency?

## NOT THE SOCIAL GOSPEL

The Care Effect ministries of FBNO are a product of and a manifestation of the gospel of Jesus Christ. But they are not an illustration of the social gospel.

These ministries are an effort to mimic the life and work of Jesus of Nazareth who was powerful in "word and deed" (Luke 24:19) and to follow the instructions of Scripture in devoting ourselves to a life of "love and good deeds" (Hebrews 10:24).

Pastors are taught that the Sunday School is the church organized for outreach and ministry:

> Just as every successful coach has a game plan, successful churches have systematic game plans to fulfill the Great Commission. The 21st century church need not reinvent the methodological wheel to look for an organizational strategy. Sunday School is not just an organization of the church. Sunday School is the church organized to fulfill the Great Commission.
> —DR. TIM SMITH, "DEVELOP A GAME PLAN: ORGANIZE YOUR CHURCH THROUGH SUNDAY SCHOOL"

This is a core teaching among Southern Baptists. Our church continues to reach people through what we call "small groups" that are really Sunday School with a new name. I continue to be a strong advocate of such work in our churches.

But not at the expense of the Great Commandment. We should include in our definition of a "successful" church some measurable demonstration of loving our neighbor. Ministry structure should be intentional about the Great Commission *and* the Great Commandment.

The commands of Scripture regarding care for the needy are certainly directed to individual believers. These commands are also frequently aimed at the church as a body (see 1 Timothy 5). Churches have organized themselves for evangelism and discipleship around the Great Commission (Matthew 28:18–20). Where is the plan to accomplish the Great Commandment?

Our preference to fulfill the Great Commission rather than the Great Commandment looks and sounds self-serving to many people both within and outside of the churches. Absent the gospel proclamation embodied in deeds of compassion, we seem to be vigorously recruiting new members because we need more bodies and money to count.

Loving our neighbors is costly. It is work. It places great demands on us personally and on our institutions.

But it is the central command of Jesus, the summation of all others. And it is not accomplished automatically when we implement the Great Commission. Loving our neighbors includes telling them about Jesus. But that is not all there is to it. If you are under that false impression, you need to revisit the parable of the Good Samaritan and all the teachings of Jesus. Love of neighbor begins in the Old Covenant with caring for strangers, widows, and orphans. It continues through the New Testament in that same vein.

Love of neighbor is not only the Great Commandment. It also encompasses the Great Commission. Any insistence on separating these two is misguided and will inevitably warp the presentation of the gospel.

A lopsided presentation of the gospel and of the Savior—a Great Commission without a Great Commandment—actually undercuts evangelism and discipleship. It doesn't look or sound true because it is not true to Jesus Himself or the gospel He came to incarnate and proclaim. John the Baptist's question about Jesus is perennial: "Are you the one?" (Luke 7:20). The answer Jesus gave included good deeds as well as good words: "Go back and report to John what you have seen and heard: The blind receive sight, the lame walk, those who have leprosy are cleansed, the deaf hear, the dead are raised, and the good news is proclaimed to the poor" (Luke 7:22).

We have a Savior whose works of compassion are beyond famous. Loving deeds permeate the popular perceptions of Jesus because they permeated the person and work of Jesus. These deeds of compassion are embedded in the languages of the earth through references to the Good Samaritan, the lost sheep, the prodigal son, the Beatitudes, etc. No presentation of the Savior is complete without them.

The church presents a misshapen and anemic gospel if it is not incarnating the love of God through love of neighbor.

The Care Effect is our effort at FBNO to proclaim the full-orbed gospel of Christ with both word and deed.

Words are not enough. Absent the deeds, they will not satisfy this new generation no matter how powerful the apologetic may be. Words have never been enough. That is why God became flesh.

Our greatest apologetic is the incarnation of God's love through deeds of compassion. We cannot uncouple words from deeds. It is an artificial, unhelpful, and finally detrimental distinction.

Loving neighbors has always been costly in time and resources. Some pastors insist that churches cannot afford to do such work, that the needs are too great. Loving neighbors, however, has always been a selective process. We do the work that God puts in our path and in our hearts, whatever the cost. God will show us our particular assignment if we will ask him.

We need a theory and practice of church that includes the Great Commandment. Fulfilling the Great Commandment should be in our budget, in our staff assignments, and on our weekly church calendar. Our churches need to be famous for love and good deeds.

Then we will look and sound much more like our winsome, wonderful Savior.

## REFLECTIONS

1. What is the Great Commission? What is its scriptural basis?
2. What is the Great Commandment? What is its scriptural basis?
3. How are these two related?
4. How would one faithfully accomplish one of these without also doing the other?

## DON'T PIT MEMBER CARE AGAINST OUTSIDER CARE

We live in a mental world that insists on "either/or." Given that resources are limited, convinced that ideologies are conflicting, we think either we can do this or do that, but we cannot do both. We hold this either/or mentality about compassion ministries and evangelism.

We think we cannot do both. But the fact is, we must do both. We have no choice as followers of Jesus.

So our either/or mentality is a falsehood, a lie. Jesus commands both love for our neighbor *and* evangelism. They cannot be mutually exclusive. Thinking so is just another way of avoiding His clear command.

We may try to apply this either/or mentality to addressing the needs of others. We think our church must choose between helping its own members or helping persons in the community, but it cannot do both. We pretend that these two activities are mutually exclusive, even in our own lives. We may commit ourselves personally to helping our own members and deliberately exclude the stranger from our circle of care.

Once again, we are under a false impression. This dichotomy, too, is a lie.

Love for one another in the church does not trump love of neighbor, love of strangers, or love of our enemies. These loves are all compatible, and all are part of the same movement of our hearts. We cannot really do one without doing the other. This is the distinctive nature of *agape*, the Father's love for us and our subsequent love for Him and for others.

The Apostle Paul bleeds these two dimensions of the same love together in Romans 13:8. He begins the sentence with "love one another" and ends it with "he who loves his fellowman" (Weymouth New Testament). Is he talking about loving church members or loving neighbors? In the next sentence, verse 9, he quotes "Love your neighbor as yourself."

Our hardworking volunteers consistently deliver 20–30 hot meals every Wednesday, mostly to our own members. Those meal boxes contain fresh-baked cookies as well as a meat and vegetables. In fact, our homebound members enjoy the same meal that we enjoy at the church fellowship hall.

This ministry of meal delivery is both costly and rewarding. Volunteers depart the church property to make multiple stops during drive time on congested streets. They burn their own gas and drive their own vehicles. They serve others in the family of faith at significant cost in time and money.

And they do it 52 weeks a year.

Our ministry to church members in need has never been as strong as it is today. We distribute tens of thousands of dollars to address the needs within our church family. In all my years as a pastor I have never come close to such a level of practical care for those within the membership.

This level of internal care is occurring at the same time as the level of care for those beyond the walls has peaked both in terms of volunteers and financial investment. This is made possible both through the regular tithes and offerings of our congregation and through partnerships with other churches and entities.

A different perspective on those outside the walls might help our mental struggle. Strangers are only friends we haven't met yet. Outsiders are pre-membership, not non-membership.

When we relocated the facilities of FBNO, we did so for the benefit of people we had never met, whose faces we had never seen. We did not do it for ourselves. We were all happy, more or less, with the way things were. If it was just "us four and no more," then relocation was completely unnecessary.

The desire to receive neighbors who were not yet friends drove the relocation of our church facilities. And the desire to love and receive strangers drives the Care Effect. For us, both of these were motivated by love beyond the walls.

Pastors and church members do not need to choose between helping those within and those outside the church. The Bible commands both. We cannot ignore either. If we do one effectively and consistently, we will be drawn to do the other as well. Love knows no bounds. Love compels us toward the need wherever it may be.

This is true even when resources are limited, as they always are. Somehow love finds expression in the spheres that Christ identifies and commands as incumbent on His church.

## ARTICULATE THE MISSION

Hannah Pounds is a young mother and physician, the chief medical director of Baptist Community Health Services (BCHS) in the Lower Ninth Ward of New Orleans. Our local Baptist association launched this ministry of compassion in 2014. Hannah could have easily landed a better-paying job, but she chooses to spend her time helping the hurting in this medically under-served area of our city. This is her calling from God, she says, and she came to realize it as she grew up in our church doing missions at home and abroad.

"How would you articulate the mission of our clinic?" she asked. Hannah is eloquent—a great presenter. But she wanted to refine and enrich the talking points and the vocabulary of her message.

We walked as we talked. We are disciples in motion, and I need the exercise.

Physicians, along with all kinds of professionals and caregivers, may be passionately committed to Christ. As such, they are determined to do their work, not to please men, but to please God. They feel called to their vocation, but sometimes they wonder how their particular mission fits into the overall mission of the church of Jesus Christ. They want to understand this for themselves and be able to explain it to others.

We are most enthusiastic about our good work when we understand clearly the biblical foundation and the motivation for our work. Every individual and team who seeks to represent Christ in deeds of compassion should give time and attention to the scriptural support for the work. Crafting a mission statement helps us crystallize these things in our own minds as well as communicate them to others.

Hannah talked about how God should receive the glory from our work. That is why we let our light shine, Jesus said, "that they may see your good deeds and glorify your Father in heaven" (Matthew 5:16). We bring God glory when we make it clear that our love for Christ motivates us to be present in the pain.

I have been invited to help with the dedication of many Habitat houses. Each time I tell the gathered crowd that we are followers of

Jesus, and that is why we are present. I realize as I say this that some of those helping build houses are there for other reasons.

The teaching of Jesus concerning the blind man (John 9:2–3) is a great place to begin writing a mission statement for any ministry or organization that is established through faith in Christ with the goal of helping those in need. The blind man's affliction was present so that the glory of God might be displayed in him. We bring glory to God by exalting His name and highlighting His work in the world through our words and deeds.

A mission statement might begin with, "The mission of this ministry is to bring glory to God . . ."

A hammer follows the same arc whether you are swinging it for Jesus or swinging it for humanitarian concerns. A physician who follows Jesus takes blood pressure the same way any physician would do it. The actual event of care by a Christian may not be distinguishable from the care given by any person in that situation.

How do we light up our work so that people give God the glory?

God's Word is the light of the world (see John 1). Our word is also our light. When we give care to others, that good deed is center stage. In the process of giving care we must somehow explain our connection to the Father through Jesus His Son. Our words turn on the spotlight that lights up our works.

Deeds of compassion should always be connected to the gospel narrative. Words and deeds go together in the Christian life and in the proclamation of the gospel. That is how God gets the glory.

I was privileged to participate in numerous home dedications as part of our home-building and home-renewal ministries. Each time I announced to those present, "I am here because Jesus is Lord, and His love compels me to care for those around me." I did not assume that this truth was self-evident.

Good works are always an effort to "love your neighbor." We must all operate in love every day. This is how we grow to be more like Christ and experience the maturation of our faith.

Thousands of volunteers reported for duty in the aftermath of Hurricane Katrina. They came to swing hammers, man shovels, and carry mountains of debris to the curb for pickup. I always told them, "Swing your hammers with love in your hearts for those homeowners. Scoop that muck with love in your hearts for one another. Without love, we're just burning calories. When others know that you love them, you maximize your kingdom impact."

This is the core of my response to Hannah and to all who ask us how and why we do our good work. We seek to express the love of Christ. We pay that love forward. We obey the command to love.

Love is an essential ingredient in any ministry that wishes to represent Christ in the world. Without love we are simply clanging cymbals or noisy gongs, and we gain nothing (1 Corinthians 13). Christian ministry is all about love. Often when our Care Effect teams are about to deploy into the field I offer a prayer for them. My prayer usually includes something like this: "Help us serve every person with heartfelt love so that our work will have its maximum spiritual effect."

So we could expand the mission statement to read, "Our mission is to bring God glory and to love our neighbors by . . . "

A mission statement for BCHS might read like this: "Baptist Community Health Services is a nonprofit community-based health care provider that serves the primary care needs of residents in under-served areas in order to bring glory to God and express the love of Christ."

The mission statement, once formulated, may need to be accompanied by a mission-appropriate list of objectives that hardwire the deeds of compassion to the good news about Christ. At BCHS, this mean Christian literature is readily available, and pastors and chaplains are also available to patients who desire a visit.

Hannah asks each patient if she can pray with them. This is one way in which God's presence and a Christian's purpose can be immediately made known to those in need. This is true whether or not the person in need affirms the prayer.

Our good work is not predicated upon the person in need's response to the gospel. That would truly empty the good deed of all its love. If loving concern for the sick is suspended because it does not result in enough baptisms or church plants, then the community realizes that our good deeds are utilitarian—that we only perform the good deed if we get the right response. This kind of mindset undercuts the gospel itself. In the developing world it may result in what missionaries sometimes call "rice Christians." They identify themselves as Christians in order to receive the rice. Having received it, they go back immediately to their true faith or lack thereof.

Genuine faith in Christ cannot be coerced, even gently. A child in poverty may desire desperately to please the caregiver, to give that caregiver what he wants to see and let him hear what he wants to hear. We cannot really solve this problem, but we can be sensitive to its reality and make sure that our love is not contingent upon a religious response that we desire. Jesus did not incorporate such a condition upon His own good work, and He did not instruct us to do it. Our reward is from God, not from people.

The clinic staff prays together and seeks to maintain a culture of care linked to faith in Christ. Daily operations are immersed in the gospel message. The link between the clinic and our churches is clear. The presence of the clinic when deliberately connected to our churches becomes evidence to the larger community of our care for others and the goodness of God.

Clarify the purpose of your compassion ministries with a mission statement that is easily remembered by volunteers and staff alike. Work on the wording. Rehearse it frequently. Good deeds have the greatest gospel effect when the purpose is crystal clear.

## REFLECTIONS

1. What Bible passages come to mind when you think about the mission of compassion ministries?
2. What would you include in a mission statement for a ministry that administered health care?

3. Write a mission statement, no more than two sentences, that would hard-wire deeds of love with the proclamation of the gospel.

4. What spiritual outcomes do you expect from a ministry of compassion?

# DON'T GIVE UP

The thieves were untying the wire mesh from the poles when we drove up. Dolores slammed on the brakes and jumped out of the car. She was screaming.

"Get away from that fence!" she cried. "Thieves! That's my fence!" The thieves looked up, somewhat concerned, dropped their hands to their sides, and sauntered away down the mountain and out of sight.

Dolores was livid. She slid back behind the steering wheel, muttering to herself.

"They steal everything," she said. "It's part of their culture. They love to sneak around you and trick you and take what isn't theirs."

She sat still, staring toward the mountain peaks that surrounded us. "I built these gardens, a dozen of them. I wanted them to learn how to be gardeners." Her voice trailed off.

"They steal everything. This was the only garden left that wasn't vandalized. They take all the fencing."

"These are your Christians," she said, animated again and rising in the car seat. "They lie and steal. They say they are Christians just so they can go to Timika and drink and chase women." Timika was a city on the coast of Papua built by the mining company as a port for the export of copper and gold.

She sat back again, limp and tired. "I don't know what to do. They have no gardens in their culture." Again her voice trailed off and she stared into space.

I sat silently, waiting for her to complete her train of thought.

"Their diet is deficient, you know," she continued, glancing over at me, "mostly yams and hardly any protein. That's why their hair turns orange." I had seen the strange orange tint to their hair. I knew their life expectancy was still about 40 years.

"I don't know how to help them," she said with a sigh, calming down. "I've been here 30 years, and still I don't know how to help them."

She threw up her hands, literally. "I'm giving up," she said. "I'm going home."

Dolores came to Papua with all the idealism of a young person determined to change the world. She knew I was a Christian pastor from the United States. She was showing us around the island as a favor to our host in Papua.

I was sitting in her jeep when Dolores announced that she was giving up. I heard firsthand her comments about the Papuans. I didn't know if Dolores was speaking out of frustration or with the real intention to return to her homeland. But I knew that God was trying to teach me something through it all.

Followers of Jesus came to Papua a generation ago to share the love of Christ. They died on the Papuan missions field, killed by cannibals. If we remain faithful to our Lord who died on the Cross, we don't ever give up. Jesus didn't give up on us, and we don't give up on others.

I thought of John Cutts, missionary to the Papuans and a man of tremendous energy and passion for Christ. He walked these precipitous trails day after day. He lived in stark conditions when he could easily have pulled out and gone to America. He invested his life helping the Papuans, giving them the gospel, and did it with great determination and joy.

Any person doing good, giving care, is subject to discouragement. So I don't want to fault Dolores for her frustration. I have felt a similar frustration in the work I do as a pastor.

But I do believe that the Holy Spirit must be our enabler in the good work we do. We must tap into divine resources. We do not have sufficient personal resources to sustain us when the rewards seem meager and the suffering escalates. Our hope is always in God who equips and sustains us in the work He calls us to do.

## THE GRAY RIVER

A gray river flows from the heights of the mountains in Papua, beginning at 11,000 feet. It plunges off the steep slopes, through the crevasses and canyons, and 80 miles later arrives at the sea. It widens as it courses toward the coast until it is a vast expanse of gray.

The concentrators in the copper mining operation at Grasberg pulverize the ore that arrives by truck and belt. The mine employs lime mixed with water in a succession of tanks to separate the gold and copper from the rock and soil. This process is only able to lift 97 percent of the gold out of the raw ore. The rest of the gold is discharged into the river that gets its gray color from the crushed rock discharged from the concentrators.

Indigenous Papuans have discovered that they can separate the gold from the worthless silt by panning. Like figures in Dante's *Inferno*, many individuals may be spied, straining against the current of the water at their knees or waist, caked with gray silt, working their equipment, panning for gold.

A man named Daniel was present with us at the missionary house one night in the mountains of Papua. I preached that evening in the village of Pogapa. After the time of worship we ate together and then began to visit. Daniel, a native of Papua, is a small man with a quick wit and a great intellect. He listened to our conversation with interest.

We talked about his work among many churches in Papuan villages. Daniel was district superintendent for dozens of churches planted by the Christian and Missionary Alliance missionaries. The Alliance structure is more Methodist than Baptist in that pastors are appointed to serve in a church for a certain term.

I asked him what his prayer requests might be, given the challenges of his position.

"Pray that our pastors will not leave their churches to go and pan for gold," he responded immediately.

A pastor's salary in Papua is about $100 per month. An industrious man panning for gold may make ten times that much. The practice is illegal and dangerous, but the government cannot seem to prevent it.

Some pastors have left their churches to pan for gold. The problem is common enough to become the chief prayer request of Daniel. Papuan pastors must be willing to live on meager salaries if they are to stay true to their calling. The gold mine has made it possible to achieve great financial gain in a world where only rich people make $1,000 a month.

I suspect that some pastors, as well as other Christians, in all places and all times have abandoned their churches to metaphorically pan for gold. Exceptions can be cited, but normally pastors don't get rich. Laying down your life for Christ is expensive. You only do it when you know for certain that you have found the pearl of great price, worth more than all the other things people treasure.

Papua is now strung between its former standard of subsistence living and a new standard of industrial jobs and much higher income. How does it affect a pastor and his family to shun the gray river and pay all the bills on $100 a month? One can appreciate the strength of such a temptation.

None of these answers come easily. Maybe there are no firm answers, only immediate responses to evident needs. But the spiritual and financial development of the Papuan people and their churches may afford one of the most significant missions opportunities of our time.

Evangelicals, including Southern Baptists, developed the Christian work in Papua. We have a tremendous responsibility to continue the proclamation and incarnation of the gospel in this part of the world where Christian meets Muslim every day. This strategic witness touches the largest Muslim nation in the world, Indonesia. And it will only be maximized through continued investment from brothers and sisters abroad. We must be willing to address the evident humanitarian needs and stay engaged as the Papuan Christians, their pastors, and their churches journey toward spiritual maturity, economic stability, and modern health care.

## PATIENCE AND DETERMINATION

I did some combat fishing in the Russian River on the Kenai Peninsula in Alaska a few years ago. Combat fishing happens when everyone fishes in the same spot. The red salmon were still running, and the silver salmon had just begun to come up the river. People were almost shoulder-to-shoulder.

I had been using the same fishing rod for several days, and it was not working right. Sometimes the reel would lock after I cast and sometimes it wouldn't. So I was using my thumb to control the spool of line and doing pretty well. I had landed some fish.

I worked my way into the middle of the pack. Instead of fishing near the bank, I fished at the very point where the clear waters of the Russian River meet the gray waters of the Kenai River. Glacial water is easily identified by its color, and the Kenai is certainly fed by glaciers. The two streams of water run side by side as a single river for several hundred yards, the left side being clear and the right gray. The fishermen were lined up in the clear water where they could watch the salmon swimming by and the fish could spot the lures.

Baby ducks wove their way in and out among the fishermen. Huge white gulls picked the bloody skeletons of recently filleted fish. And I dragged my single hook fly through the water over and over again, hoping to snag a big one in the mouth.

Instead of snagging one, however, I actually hooked one that went after the fly. I saw a flash of silver as he churned in the water, and then I saw my line heading downstream. That line was 25-pound test line. I had tied the fly with multiple knots. The line was not going to break. But my spool was not locking. The line was spinning away. I pushed my thumb down to stop the whining spool and burned a blister on my thumb. I tried to reel, but the fish was too big and strong. He just kept stripping line off the spool.

Fishermen began to jump back and curse as my line got tangled with theirs. I slogged through the stream to the bank, water running over my wading boots, and tried again to hold the fish. I couldn't hold him. He was 50 yards downstream now, and every fisherman between me and the fish was beginning to tangle up in my line.

I tried to reel him in once more, but he was still running. Only a small amount of line was left on the whole spool. If he ripped it to the end I would be out of fishing for the day, my youth minister's new fishing line all gone.

With my pole bent double, I cried out down the bank, "Someone down there cut the line for me."

And someone did. A fisherman stepped off the bank and into the water, grabbed my line with one hand, and clipped it with a knife in the other hand.

The episode of the monster salmon has become one of two troublesome sports memories, the other being the time in Mississippi when a massive buck with huge antlers almost ran over me in the woods, and I wasn't ready.

I woke up the next morning at 1:30 thinking about that fish. When I yelled, "Cut the line!" I thought it was the gracious and sensible thing to do. In retrospect, however, I wish that I had thrown down that useless rod, grabbed the line with my bare hands, and hauled that monster in. It would have been a scene like one in Hemingway's *The Old Man and the Sea*. I should have stayed with that salmon as he towed me down the shoreline. I should have wrapped that line around my body and pulled hand over hand. Finally, with bloody hands and a tangled mass of line, I might have landed that feisty fish. Probably not. But maybe. At least I wouldn't have had to worry about the wisdom of cutting the line.

I lay in the bed for a long while, unable to sleep. And I asked the Lord, "Why can't I get this silly fish out of my head?" Maybe I am supposed to learn something from that fish, I thought, so I asked myself: "Are you the kind of man who cuts the line when things get tough?" Now I really had food for thought.

The big ones usually get away, not because they outfox us, but because they outlast us. The big ones get away, not because we lack the skill to win, but because we lack the will to win. The big ones often get away, not because we are too weak, but because we quit too soon.

It is always easier to cut the line. You are not absolutely certain that you can land that fish anyway. You have folks around you upset because your big project has interrupted their plans. They don't think you can get the job done, and you are doubtful. Too often when the going gets tough, we cut the line.

No wonder Jesus called at least four fishermen to be His closest disciples. Successful fishermen must cultivate two qualities that serve us all well in every area of life—patience and determination. The two are closely related. Patience is the ability to wait until the fish start biting, and the ability to bring them in slowly so you do not rip the hook out. Determination keeps you in the stream when the current is swift, when the fishing is slow, when the crowds are thick, and when the "big one" hits the line.

Yes, there is a time to call it quits, a time when the investment exceeds any possibility of return. Dogged determination may become simple stubbornness. Like the Old Man in *The Old Man and the Sea*, sometimes "the big one" does tow us too far out to sea. We must be determined, and we must be wise.

Compassion ministries demand a lot of us and of our churches. They may be expensive in time and money. We have had to develop three independent funding streams outside of our regular tithes and offerings to sustain the large projects in which we are engaged. Developing partnerships has become a key practice.

Let's not cut the line too quickly, however. God has big projects for each of us to do. None of them will be accomplished without patience and determination. All of them will place great demands on our personal energy and the resources at our disposal. These projects are great, not only in their demand but also in their impact. They bear witness to the love of Christ before an entire community.

Many works of compassion are time-bound endeavors. They are initiated in God's time, and they are terminated in God's time. The ability to shut down what is no longer working is just as important as the ability to start up a new ministry that addresses a new need.

And remember, everybody loses a few big ones. You cannot lose sleep over lost fish.

## REFLECTIONS

1. Are you now launching, or have you ever launched, something you consider "big"?
2. What kinds of demands did this big project make on you?
3. Does patience come easy for you?
4. Have you ever cut the line too soon?

## COMPASSION MINISTRIES MAY BE EXHAUSTING

Our church deploys 100 volunteers each week into our needy community. These volunteers bear their own burdens even as they reach out to help others. They deal with sickness themselves, and grief. Some have financial woes. Others have wayward children and grandchildren. They are busy people with many demands on their time. And they make room in their lives for neighbors with needs.

This is a deliberate choice. Any one of us could close down and focus only on our own problems, our own family. We are all tempted to walk quickly past the hurting person on the other side of the road (Luke 10:32). We know how complicated helping can be. We know that it demands more time than we think we have.

Loving neighbors is a costly thing to do.

Therefore, caring for others requires and will develop certain qualities of character in the caregiver.

And giving care sometimes takes the caregiver to the limits of all personal resources.

*We want each of you to show this same diligence to the very end, so that what you hope for may be fully realized.*

163

*We do not want you to become lazy, but to imitate those who through faith and patience inherit what has been promised.*

—HEBREWS 6:11–12

*You need to persevere so that when you have done the will of God, you will receive what he has promised.*

—HEBREWS 10:36

## LIMITING OUT ON PERSONAL RESOURCES

My parents lost their home to a fire in the winter of their 45th year together.

A young physician rushed to their assistance the night of the fire. He just wanted to help. My parents and their 16-year-old son, Matthew, stood beside the smoldering ashes in the cold, having only the clothes on their back.

Matthew wore a T-shirt. He had no coat. The physician noticed him shivering, so he took off his light jacket and draped it around Matthew's shoulders. Then he turned to my father and asked what else he could do to help.

My father glanced down at the young physician's trousers, and asked him what size his pants were. The young man was startled and tongue-tied for a minute, until he realized that Dad was teasing him.

A sense of humor is one of God's great gifts. Every caregiver needs it, from the obstetrician to the undertaker.

Dad took the fire in stride. The house was so full of old furniture one could hardly navigate through it, and mother could still not pass up a good deal at a rummage sale. Is your mother like this? Dad mumbled his objections for years. He decided the fire was divine intervention to cut down on the junk.

This was actually the second home my parents lost to fire. The first came in 1952, the year before I was born. Their small mobile home burned with their few worldly possessions. They were college students at the time, and the Bible college helped them recover from their loss. Interestingly, one of the charred photographs pulled from the ashes of the house fire was of that burned-out trailer they lost 42 years earlier.

Mother grieved the loss of thousands of pictures, but Dad claimed we never looked at them anyway.

Remembrances of fires and floods dim and eventually pass out of all memory. Our belongings are temporary. The very records of their existence are also temporary. Dollar bills and coins pass through our hands and are gone. The entire matter of purchase, transaction, acquisition, and disposal disappears into the mist of time. Eventually even the planet we live on will be renovated by fire, and all signs of human fingerprints, footprints, and glossy prints will be burned away. So says earthy Peter, the Lord's right hand man (2 Peter 3:10–11). Jesus, working from a heavenly perspective, encouraged us to work for the bread that lasts forever (John 6:27).

Given this truth, only a true materialist would give his or her life completely to acquisition and consumption.

Caring for others offers temporal and eternal reward. But it can be taxing, exhausting work. People can "become weary in doing good" (Galatians 6:9). Sometimes our care is given to persons in their sunset years when we know that physical healing is not likely.

We may be overwhelmed by the demands of our mission and the human need around us. Sometimes our internal resources run dry.

## FORCES THAT PUSH US AWAY
## FROM COMPASSION MINISTRIES

I have felt the pressure, internal and external, to abandon a focus on the second commandment, "love your neighbor as yourself" (Mark 12:31), and turn my attention elsewhere. What are these forces that seem to push us away from the second commandment? I can identify a few.

First, we believe in salvation by grace through faith in the Lord Jesus Christ. We do not believe that good works can save us. A focus on good deeds may be misunderstood or misrepresented as salvation by works.

Second, we who are professional Christians, so to speak, are heirs of the Reformation. We love theology and theological debate. We are philosophical, intellectual, and reasonable creatures. We tend to favor the world of words and ideas. We want to love God with our minds. This is a comfortable focus for us.

Third, as evangelicals we believe that Scripture is infallible and inerrant. Therefore, we tend to be scribal in our leanings. We tend to reduce our obligations to the study and communication of words oral and written. We are "people of the Book," as we should be, and we have taken that to mean that 99 percent of our responsibility before God is about the treatment of words on the page.

Fourth, we are guardians of massive religious institutions. Those institutions require great resources. When we think about the expenditure of church funds, we are pressed to provide for personnel, denominational needs, and building costs. Every budget represents a compromise between competing interests. The love of neighbor could get expensive even for the church.

Fifth, we are frightened of any association with the "social gospel" of a hundred years ago that really had no good news in it—only good deeds. We want to be known as faithful followers of Jesus who believe in His death, burial, and Resurrection, not as "do-gooders" who have abandoned true faith in Christ. For the record, I am evangelical in my theology. I lead people to trust Christ as Savior and Lord. I have no interest in a philanthropic lifestyle alone. I want to be more like Jesus, and that desire pushes me toward the second commandment.

Sixth, we are no more comfortable with the definition and parameters of "neighbor" than the expert in the law. This commandment intimidates us, as well it should.

Perhaps the best approach to reintroducing the second commandment is to follow the lead of Jesus in identifying our neighbors.

## REFLECTIONS

1. How does our keeping of the second commandment, to love our neighbor, indicate our keeping of the first, to love God?
2. Would you agree that discussions about good deeds are sometimes uncomfortable for grace-oriented people?
3. Is there any possibility that our administration of God's resources has been warped by self-interest? How could that happen?


# THE HOUSE BURNED BECAUSE THE WELL RAN DRY

I learned something recently that I should have known for many years. My parents' home burned to the ground because the well ran dry.

Many homes in rural areas are connected to rural water company systems. Theirs was connected to an old and shallow well. My brother Danny was using the water one day when the well ran dry. He said the water would flow at full volume for about 30 minutes before the reservoir was empty.

Firefighters speculated that the fire began because a spark from the wood-burning stove escaped up the chimney and came back down on the roof. It found a crevasse between shingles, and lodged against the wooden decking. It was a windy day, and the spark was fanned into a flame.

The fire crept from the roof decking down into the attic. When they realized what was happening, Dad opened the attic door and found the attic ablaze. He ran a water hose into that attic and, standing on a ladder with his head and shoulders in the attic, began to douse the fire. Mother was on the phone with the fire department describing what she saw. When she told them that Dad was halfway in the attic, they told her to get him out of there. Mother could not convince Dad to stop spraying the flames in the attic. I doubt he would have come down even for the firefighters.

But he did come down out of the attic and off that ladder—in about 30 minutes. He was actually defeating the fire, he insisted, when the water hose went limp and the flow of water stopped.

The reservoir was empty. The well had run dry. That's when the fire took over and destroyed their home.

Danny gave me this account of the fire in casual conversation only a couple of years ago. He thought I knew, but somehow this part of the story escaped me.

I can see my father running for the water hose and dragging it into the house. I can see him standing on a ladder or some piece of furniture, his upper body in the attic, spraying that stream full blast at the flames.

Dad was never one to retreat from the flames.

I set the yard on fire one day. It was a very dry summer. Wildfires were reported all around the farm. We boys heard a rumor that a pasture was ablaze just north of our house.

I told my brothers that it would be smart to burn off the tall grass that crept near our house in the valley. That way our house would be protected should the wildfire come over the ridge and into our valley.

They were persuaded, and we got some matches and started a fire in grass three feet tall. It moved quickly, climbing up those dry stems, and got hotter than we anticipated. In minutes the fire was roaring, spreading in three directions. We got the water hose, but the fire was already beyond the reach of the spray.

Suddenly our father arrived armed with a wet towel in each hand. He waded into the flames. We watched helplessly as he battled the fire by himself. We stood between the house and the fire with our mouths wide open. We knew how hot that fire was, and we just couldn't believe that he was in the middle of it.

He was a thumping, swinging, wild windmill of a man. Alone, he beat the fire into submission and then into extinction.

When his wet towels had smothered the last flame and scattered the last sparks, he straightened his back and dropped his arms to his sides. He was out of breath, exhausted.

He turned and strode quickly out of the black circle of burnt grass. He took the garden hose out of my hands and doused himself from head to foot. He smelled like smoke and scorched hair. The fire trimmed his eyebrows and burned the thick black hair off his arms.

This event confirmed the suspicions of his wide-eyed boys. Dad really was a superhero.

So if my father said he was gaining on the flames and would have put out the fire had the well not run dry, I have to believe him.

Sometimes you just run out of water, even if you're a superhero. Your reservoir of physical, spiritual, and emotional resources just dries up. It's not anyone's fault. It's not moral failure. Human resources are finite, limited. Humans cannot do anything endlessly, without rest, without renewal.

Caregivers are often at risk of giving beyond their resources without knowing they are doing so. Our souls run dry, and we wonder what's wrong with us.

Disaster will stretch you to your limits, then take you past those limits before you know it. I felt that sensation of the dry well many times during the aftermath of Hurricane Katrina. While driving through the country on the way to see family or friends, I would suddenly experience a tremendous sense of relief and release, as if I had driven out of a thick fog or dropped an enormous burden off my shoulders. I didn't realize until that moment that I was even in a fog or feeling burdened.

I am grateful for the people who knew that we needed breaks— and brakes—in that grueling routine of disaster recovery. They cared for us in the midst of our care for others. They helped us find refreshment for our souls and ministry for our own needs.

Who cares for the caregivers?

Needy people pursued Jesus. They were relentless and demanding. They did not appreciate who He was. Some of them never really understood the point of all He did. They only wanted the bread. They wanted Him to heal them. They carried their loved ones to His feet and plead for a miracle.

The crowd surrounded Him, loud and boisterous, and He cared for them. He fed them and healed their sick.

And He pulled aside often to escape the demands of the noisy crowd and find refreshment for His soul. Jesus would find a secluded place, all alone, and pray. He discovered in communion with His Father all the resources He needed to step into the fray again the next day. This pulling away, dropping out of sight, was characteristic of Him.

In part, Jesus did it for us, so we would not feel guilty when we had to get away. In your mind you can see Jesus in the middle of a needy crowd. Now picture Him ascending to the Father, straight up into the sky. And picture yourself in Jesus' place in the center of that crowd.

Jesus ascended, and He left the crowd of needy people with us. This is what it means to follow Him, to be His disciple. You will be cognizant of overwhelming need, surrounded by people in trouble. You will help them, pray for them, feed them, and bind up their wounds.

And sometimes you will be exhausted, and you will need to escape. Your well will run dry.

Fire turns photographs to ashes. Fire turns appliances into junk metal. Fire transforms kitchenware into puddles of colorful plastic.

But some things last forever. Jesus taught us how to put it all in perspective. "Whoever wants to be my disciple must deny themselves and take up their cross and follow me" (Matthew 16:24). The greatest in the kingdom is the servant of all.

Remember, "The only thing that counts is faith expressing itself through love" (Galatians 5:6).

## REFLECTIONS

1. Are you currently a caregiver for someone? Have you ever been?
2. Do you remember a time when your personal internal resources were simply depleted?
3. How do you find new strength when all your strength is gone?
4. Do you ever "become weary in doing good"?

SUMMARY

# Doing What
# We Know

TWO FOSTER CHILDREN, BROTHERS AGES FOUR AND FIVE, SAW me in the church lobby. Their foster father asked them who I was. They pointed at me and yelled out loud, "The pizza man!"

I made an impression the evening I delivered supper to this foster family. I called the foster parents, Andrew and Allye, and told them I was bringing dinner.

"Would pizza be OK?" I asked.

"Oh, yes," they said, relieved that dinner was provided that day. "The boys love pizza." The boys were foster children who had been in their care for a couple of months.

I rang the doorbell, and the foster children gathered at the door along with Andrew and his own daughter, Ruby, in his arms. They greeted me and took the pizza box right out of my hands.

I closed the door behind me, and the boys looked at me puzzled. Then I sat down with the family and began to enjoy the pizza with them.

One of the foster boys looked at me curiously. He couldn't figure me out.

"Why are you staying?" he asked. The pizza man always delivered the pizza and left.

So I became the pizza man to these two boys who attended our church for nearly a year before being adopted.

This glorious opportunity to care for orphans was provided for me as a pastor only because we became concerned about foster children and foster families and tried to do something about it.

We are not sure what to do with the command to love our neighbor as we love ourselves. The command is unwieldy and impossible on multiple fronts. We are not always certain what love demands, and we frequently hesitate when we count the cost.

Talk is cheap, at least in some ways. We may prefer "go tell" to "go and do likewise." We may prefer Bible study to Bible implementation. All believers are tempted to do this. We become hearers only instead of doers.

Our concern for orthodoxy—right doctrine—may overwhelm our concern for orthopraxy—right practice. Our need for intellectual and philosophical consistency might displace the need for simple obedience to Jesus' clear command.

We are following Jesus. We are not primarily citizens of any particular nation-state. We are not primarily members of any clan or tribe. We are not primarily defined by our vocation or profession. We are not primarily Baptist or Catholic. These labels and activities are temporary realities.

We are Jesus people, now and forever. We have sold everything to obtain this pearl of great price. If this does not describe us, then we are not His disciples at all, for these are the conditions under which He will receive us (see Matthew 16:24).

Following Jesus means that we, like Him, prioritize works of compassion. Jesus "went around doing good and healing all who were under the power of the devil, because God was with him" (Acts 10:38). That would be us now, His followers, "doing good and healing all."

It's time to pull out your personal calendar and your church calendar. Look over the weekly activities and circle those that are deliberately aimed at neighbors in need. If neighbors in need are not on your calendar, they may not be on your mind and heart.

Take a look at your monthly bank statement, personal and congregational. Do entries reflect a concern for neighbors in need? If not, it might be time to amend the budget. The Good Samaritan pulled out his wallet (Luke 10:35).

Listen carefully to the local news programs for reports of neighbors in need. God's glory may be displayed through His people mobilizing to serve.

The world is a big place. The need is everywhere. Stir up the hope in your heart. Roll up your sleeves and lend your heart and hands to the task.

# ALSO BY DAVID CROSBY . . .

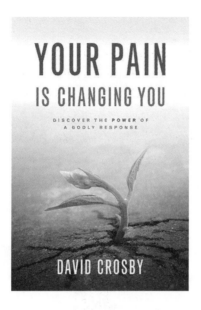

## *Your Pain Is Changing You*
Discover the Power of a Godly Response
ISBN-13: 978-1-59669-413-2 • $14.99

*Your Pain Is Changing You* does not attempt to answer the question of *why* we suffer but rather provides the *how* to persevere. David Crosby's true-life stories lead readers deep into suffering and deeper into their own theological perspective. In reading about the suffering of others, men and women will find their interest in the stories lead them to God's empowering truths. Truths that enable them to take charge of their response to pain, dramatically change their quality of life, as well as positively impact those around them. We cannot choose whether sorrow will interrupt us. We can choose our response, our character, and share that victory with others.